WILL
THERE BE
DONUTS?

WILL THERE BE DONUTS?

START A BUSINESS REVOLUTION ONE MEETING AT A TIME

DAVID PEARL

HarperCollins*Publishers*

HarperCollins*Publishers*
77–85 Fulham Palace Road,
Hammersmith, London W6 8JB

www.harpercollins.co.uk

First published in the UK by HarperCollins*Publishers* 2012
This US edition published 2013

10 9 8 7 6 5 4 3 2 1

Library of Congress Cataloging-in-Publication
Data available upon request

ISBN 978-0-00-751953-8
EBOOK ISBN 978-0-00-751954-5

Printed and bound in the United States
of America by RR Donnelley

For Joanna, Elsa, and Zachary

CONTENTS

ACKNOWLEDGEMENTS

My thanks to everyone who has kindly contributed their experiences and insights to this book.

—to Sue, Shelley, Michelle, Paul, Esperide, Kai, and the whole PG team.

—to my agent Julian Alexander, who makes the right meetings happen with the right people at the right time.

—to my editor, Nick Canham, who helped spark the revolution; Steve Burdett, who worked so hard on the manuscript; Laura Lees for the great PR; Tim Broughton for his marketing expertise; and all at HarperCollins who have made the whole experience a real pleasure.

—to my parents for providing a rich source of anecdotes, some of which they will be surprised (pleasantly, I hope!) to find featured in this book.

—to Jean and Thomas for sparking off at least one revolution.

—to Jeremy, Bruce and all the Lively Artists, as well as Phil and all at Upstage.

—to the two Davids—Glass and McCready—who've taught me more than anyone about what's really going on when human beings meet.

—and finally, to all of you everywhere who got fed up with nearly meeting and decided to start *really* meeting instead. Keep going!

FOREWORD

Back in March 2011, at the earliest stages of the book, my editor Nick Canham called a meeting. He wanted to get his colleagues at HarperCollins interested in the book; enrolled, excited. Clearly he did OK, or we wouldn't be here now. But I was curious. What was it that had brought these hardened publishing professionals to the meeting? Was it the importance of the subject? The irrefutable logic? The exquisite prose style?

I told them I'd bring donuts, said Nick.

That gave us our title. And it gives us our starting point. If the donuts are the most interesting thing about your meetings, this book is for you.

PLEASED TO MEET YOU

It's something we often say, but don't always mean. In this case I really am pleased to meet you, if only by the rather arm's-length medium of this book.

My intention in writing *Will There Be Donuts?* is to make the world a more interesting place. Or rather that you will. I am just going to help you make it fun.

And we are going to do it one great meeting at a time.

I am guessing this isn't why you picked up this book. You probably just thought if you could make the meetings you attend less dull, boring, irrelevant, and downright irritating, your life would be better. That if you could release a few hours from your working week you could be way more productive. That if the meetings you did have were genuinely helpful, inspiring even, it would be a blessing.

And you'd be right.

My point is that if we and millions of sufferers like us manage that together, we will have done more to improve the world than all those grand-sounding vision statements put together.

When you add it up—and we will—you see that there are billions of hours out there waiting to be reclaimed and turned into value.

I admit it doesn't seem a particularly glamorous or epic way to change the world. I am reminded of the final series of *The West Wing* when the old regime is coming to the end and the stalwart chief of staff CJ is being head-hunted by a Bill Gates-alike to become the new head of his humanitarian foundation. He asks her what she would do to make the world a better place. "Build highways in Africa," she blurts. With roads you can move medicines, boost productivity, increase communications, revolutionize markets. Roads aren't the glamorous answer the billionaire was expecting, but if CJ really thinks new highways will do the trick, he is willing to back her.

I feel pretty much the same way about meetings. To us as individuals they are just a feature of our daily work diary. But seen in macro they are how we exchange information, do business, invent the future, make friends, heal rifts. Doing them better is important for our businesses and for our world.

So not glamorous, but a heroic adventure nonetheless. Heroes, remember, are not extraordinary people. They are ordinary people like you and me who occasionally manage to break out of the routine and do extraordinary things.

So *will there be donuts*? It's a question being asked in offices, conferences, seminars, pitches, and presentations all over the world right now. Here are some others. See if they sound familiar. If you have found yourself asking any of these, you have come to the right place.

Is this meeting EVER going to END?

If you've ever been to a Wagner opera you know you can drift off for a nice little nap and when you wake up, nothing seems to have happened. What I call "Wagner Meetings" are the same, except the guy with the beard and the horns doesn't have a big spear but a whiteboard marker. Wagner meetings, like Wagner operas, are meant to be long. The longer they are, the more important they seem. Which is why they go on and on. Think Italian roadworks. No "work" is actually happening. They are a way of avoiding work. The whole idea is to drag things out as long as possible and then retire on a good pension before anyone notices.

Where did my day/week/year go?

Mushroom Meetings. They propagate in your diary like fungus on a rotten tree stump. Is it an airborne spore? Is it a virus? Who knows? But turn away and there they are when you open your Outlook in the morning. There are so many of them that there doesn't seem to be any room for actual work. This is particularly true in business, where any and every issue needs to be marked by a meeting. It becomes an addiction. A variation of this phenomenon is the Stonehenge Meeting. Like the stones on Salisbury Plain, they have been there since the dawn of time but no one really knows what they are for.

Is this work, or politics?

If you are wondering this, you are probably in what I call "The Party Political un-Broadcast." These meetings are like those short "infomercials" that are inserted into the TV schedule during election periods. With three important differences. These meetings are all about politics but don't warn you from the start. They aren't short. And very often the politics is not broadcast. On the contrary, it's never mentioned. But everything in the meeting is actually about political leverage and personal power-play. Oh, and one important extra difference. You can't vote these people out.

Is someone—anyone—ever going to make a decision?

Be very afraid. You are in what I call a DMZ. Like the demilitarized zone that separates North and South Korea, but far more scary. The Decision-Missing Zone. In a DMZ you'll find yourself wondering—didn't we decide this last week, and why are we talking about it again? Or why is it that we decide things in meetings and then un-decide them outside the meetings?

What am I doing here?

Welcome to the disorienting and very common Lilliput Syndrome that kicks in when meetings just aren't relevant to you. I named it after the scene in *Gulliver's Travels* where the hero (in this case you) wakes up in an alien land. It's full of little people, speaking a weird language. This world has nothing to do with you, but when you try to leave you discover you are tied down and unable to move. You're a prisoner!

This syndrome is equally common when the meeting isn't relevant to you and when you are not relevant to it!

If I covered myself in gasoline and lit a match would anyone notice?

Ah, yes, Invisible Man syndrome. They don't see you. And you cannot get your voice heard either. Partly because there's no gap in the conversation. Beware, you may be stuck in a GabFest. These are particularly popular in organizations which confuse airtime with importance and complexity with cleverness.

Are you there? Can you hear me? Hello?

They discouraged you from traveling. They increased the workload. And then they proudly introduced you to an integrated, multi-nodal tele-presence system with lots of buttons and half a mile of cable sprouting from it. Now they expect you to do real business across time zones and languages with people you've never met. But you spend your time staring into a blank screen or listening to telephone hiss ...

Did I drift off?

One client I worked with confided guiltily that he fell asleep in a meeting. I told him that was common and nothing to be ashamed of. "You don't understand," he continued. "It was a one-to-one meeting. And I was leading it!" You may not have actually bored yourself into a coma recently but, let's face it, meetings can be exceptionally and unremittingly, unremarkably, unspeakably DULL.

You wouldn't invite people to your house and bore them to death. This is partly because if your friends found you dull, they'd tell you. Or avoid you. For some reason, dullness is entirely accepted in business meetings. In some places it even passes for professionalism. It's like a piece of spinach stuck in the front teeth of Enterprise that no one's talking about. John Cleese memorably pointed out that in business people tend to confuse somber with serious—the more tedious you are, the more worthy of respect. It's an old-fashioned idea. And from what I've seen even the most serious businesses have had enough. At an event I recently organized, we asked a leadership team to help a social eco-activist clear a children's park of rocks. When I looked in on them mid-morning they were happily tossing chunks of granite to each other with their bare hands. And singing! As the CFO confided to me later, "We'd rather be in a chain gang than in a meeting."

My meetings are fine, but could they be amazing?

Well, hello there. If this is on your mind, you may be one of those rare people who don't try to *correct* their lives, but just make them *even better*, more effective/engaging/value-creating. You're not a Fixer but an Enhancer. Someone that goes to the doctor not because you are unfit, but because you want to be fitter. In a hypnosis course I once took, everyone (including me) had gone there to solve some life problem or other. All except one man. When the time came for him to state why he'd come, he blinked once or twice through his pebble glasses and asked the instructor, "Can you hypnotize me so that every time I see my wife I love her even more?" This is an Enhancer's answer.

If one or more of these situations seems familiar, I wrote this book for you.

You'll learn (in section 1) that you are not alone. Millions of people are suffering, often in silence, as poor meetings—I call them "nearly meetings"—compromise their working lives.

In section 2 we'll flip the coin and see the value of really meeting. Equipping you to really meet is what this book is about. That includes helping you understand the Anatomy of Meetings and how to design them better (in section 3), the seven essential meeting types and how to have them (section 4), and then, in section 5, we'll look at how you change meeting culture in your business and get the changes to stick without losing friends—or your job!

This is not a *how to* book in the normal sense. We already know *how to* meet. As you'll see, it's an inherent human skill. I like to think this is more of a *how NOT TO* book, reminding us to stop doing things which get in our way.

Like most smart working, better meetings are about doing less of what you know doesn't work but keep doing anyway.

Ethan Hunt: This is going to be difficult.

Mission Commander Swanbeck: Mr Hunt, this isn't mission difficult, it's mission impossible. "Difficult" should be a walk in the park for you.

Mission: Impossible II **(2001)**

I love those movie scenes where the unlikely hero, or even better a group of misfits, discover why they have been called to adventure and what their mission is. A man from covert ops with a pipe points at a map or model explaining why this has never been attempted before. Or a shadowy spymaster describes a new target on grainy film as a projector whirs in the background.

I feel we are at that point as we gather for our adventure into, around, over, and under the Weird World of Meetings.

Here is a bit of a preview of what awaits us, how to prepare, and what essentials to pack.

It's a Jungle Out There, So Stay Alert

There are lots of books on meetings which are duller than the meetings they are trying to improve. I have no intention of adding to that list.

It *is* a jungle out there. But it's a jungle of dullness.

So here's the question I'll be asking myself throughout—it works well for meetings too. *"Is this more interesting than food or sex?"*

Let me explain.

Most people I meet in business could be having more fun. One reason for this is they keep quiet when they are bored. It is considered rude to speak up or leave the room. So they suffer in silence.

It's all a lot less polite in the performing arts world I grew up in. Stand-up comedians know instantly when they have lost their audience. And if they take no notice they'll get talked over, heckled, and eventually have bottles thrown at them. That's what you call direct feedback.

It's an honorable tradition in theater.

Picture yourself in an 18th-century opera house. Opera was then what the movies are to us today—the most dramatic, sensational, sound- and music-filled experience available. And to insure it stayed that way, opera houses were constructed as a series of "boxes." One side of your box faced the stage and the other opened to drinking, dining, and wooing facilities when and if the stage action became dull. This meant opera audiences voted with their feet (and other parts of the body) if an opera failed to engage them. This resulted in operas that were eye-catchingly, heart-snaringly full of delight, intrigue, dance, storms, shipwrecks, divine skulduggery, and human frailty. It was only when theaters started to be constructed in serried rows, where it was difficult to leave when you were bored, that things started to get boring.

If we were actually meeting I'd suggest the same thing to you as I do to my clients. If anyone is going on too long, we use a thumbs-up signal which means "I got it, move on." It's visible. It's immediate. It's kinder than the hand slicing across the windpipe action that people often use to indicate you are overrunning.

As we are not in direct contact, can I just suggest that if I lose your interest, you put the book down, stretch your legs and grab a bite?* The sex thing is entirely up to you.

Despite our title I'm not sure I'd recommend a donut as a meeting snack. As the New York Obesity Research Center puts it, "The average donut is nothing more than refined sugar and flour, artificial flavors and partially hydrogenated oil that's loaded with trans fats. When it comes to health, the only thing good about them is the hole."

If I bore myself, I will do the same. Deal?

Some useful terms

Here are some words and phrases I'll be using as we voyage into Meeting Land and their meanings.

"Meetings"

I am not going to restrict the book to formal meetings of eight or so people sitting around a big wooden desk. We'll look at meetings as small as two and as large as 1500. We'll focus on live meetings but include virtual ones. A lot of my clients are wrestling with virtual meetings currently. The bottom line is that everything you need to do for a live meeting, you need to do even more for a virtual one.

"Your meetings"

When I say "your" meetings I am including those you lead and those you attend. When we look at them from the highest level (and we will) they are indeed all "your" meetings—whether they feel like it or not.

"They"

"*They*" are the people who are causing the problems. *They* are not going to read this book, which is why you will have to do it for them. *They* sat in the middle rows at school and were proud of their pencil cases. *They* are the boring folk. Not us. Let's keep it that way.

"Clients"

The ideas in this book are based on many years' working with businesses around the world. I have mentioned some people by their real names. Others I have disguised, as they are still operating as meeting revolutionaries in their organizations and I don't want to blow their cover. I will just refer to them by their first name and role, for example Ron the Consultant or Dominique the CEO. You are also going to be hearing from people outside business like Dame Barbara Stocking, the Head of Oxfam UK, the environmentalist Ashok Khosla, the scholar and activist Jim Garrison, and others. These are people with a stake in real meetings that goes beyond business and out into the world.

"Tried and tested techniques"

All the tips, tricks and tools I offer in this book have been rigorously tested in the field. Well, nearly all. I couldn't help myself. I have included some which have never been tried and could explode without warning. I know that won't bother an adventurer like you. Indeed, I am hoping you are going to go farther than I have, being more daring and experimental. Just let me know what you discover on your journey. I'll be waiting in eager anticipation for your report: david@willtherebedonuts.com.

"Business"

I refer a lot to business in this book, but that doesn't mean we need to restrict ourselves to commerce. The work here can be and has been applied to public sector organizations, government, NGOs and even schools. *Will There Be Donuts?* is relevant wherever two or more people are meeting together in a world that's getting busier by the day. In writing the book I assumed that people in business also have home lives (I know that's a bit of a bold assumption) and will find a lot of these techniques useful in personal life as well.

"The Arts"

You'll see I often refer to the Arts or Performing Arts. This is the point where I have to put up my hand (you can't see me, but it really is up) and confess I am a business outsider. That's probably why people call me into their businesses. My background is the Arts. All my life I have been involved (as performer, director, writer, producer) in creating experiences for people in music, theater, opera, TV, and film.

I didn't expect to be working in the business world, and if one of the world's leading consulting companies hadn't asked me to help them stage a spectacular operatic team-building experience in the early nineties (more of that later), I might not have been.

I have spent a couple of decades wandering around in a world I wasn't trained to understand and have discovered how wonderful it is to be an outsider on the inside. It allows you to be permanently puzzled about why perfectly normal people behave in such peculiar ways when they are at work.

People ask me, "When did you leave the performing arts?" and I answer that I didn't. To me businesses are theater and meetings are their stage. Some of the companies I know are every bit as dramatic and bloody as the schlockiest opera. Businesses run on creativity. Creative ventures need to be businesslike. Shakespeare, remember, was an astute businessman and property magnate. The worlds may appear very different, but their drives are often the same.

Stick Together

In the quintessential heist film *Ocean's Eleven* (2001), Danny (George Clooney) asks Rusty, the fixer character played by Brad Pitt, what he thinks is required to pull off the impossible casino robbery. Brad doesn't answer what, but who. "Off the top of my head, I'd say you're looking at a Boeski, a Jim Brown, a Miss Daisy, two Jethros and a Leon Spinks, not to mention the biggest Ella Fitzgerald ever."

The lesson is simple. If you are attempting something ambitious—and changing meeting culture is definitely that—then you need a diverse crew that's as determined (or insane) as you are. "Find hungry Samurai," as they say in Kurosawa's film *The Seven Samurai.*

Dorothy needed the Tin Man, Scarecrow, Lion, assorted munchkins, a couple of fairies, and a small dog to make it to Oz. Gather some like-spirited but unlike-minded allies to join you on the adventure. People who share your irritation at the way meetings are held currently and who think sufficiently differently from you to make sure you come up with some unusual solutions.

Also, if you are in a corporate setting and you are not in a leadership position, ideally you should enroll someone who is, to provide a "license to operate" and some high-level "air cover" for when you do. I encourage clients to put a "dotted line" around a few months during which people have permission to try new things and, if necessary, make mistakes without reprisal.

This doesn't mean you can't operate solo, but all good 007s have their Ms to watch their backs and their Qs to provide them with the baddy-neutralizing pen and amphibious getaway car.

What you should bring with you

In the saddle bag of the Real Meeting revolutionary you won't find posters, HR charts, or books on management. They are not interested in *knowing* about real meetings. They are determined to have them.

I like to recommend that every self-respecting Real Meeting-ista carries the following must-have pieces of equipment:

> *A chainsaw (heavy duty)*
> *One pair of pruning shears*
> *Semtex or equivalent industrial-strength plastic explosive*
> *And a glue gun*

You need something as dramatic as a chainsaw to slice through the dense undergrowth of "nearly meetings" and clear a giant hole to let the light in. Pruning shears are essential to shape and refine the few meetings you actually do have. The bad meeting habits of your colleagues are hard as concrete and have deep foundations. You'll need something as strong as Semtex to detonate those. And you need a glue gun to make sure the changes you make in meeting practice actually stick.

PLEASED TO MEET YOU

Clients who knew I was writing this book wanted me to pass on a couple of additional must-have items; this time not metaphorical ones.

> *Rubber Chicken*

Virginie was so fed up with people arriving late at her meetings she borrowed a large plastic chicken toy from her pet dog and presented it to the colleague who arrived last. The team loved the idea and a new ritual was born. Today any team member who dares to arrive after the agreed start time has to keep the chicken prominently on their office desk until the next monthly meeting as a silent and potent mark of public shame. It's a playful and effective deterrent.

> *Plastic Water Bottle (empty!)*

Recycling-minded companies are finding all sorts of uses for discarded plastic water bottles: waterproof jackets, jewelry, solar heating panels, insulation, desk tidies. Alain and Bill, two resourceful clients who both have a scientific background, discovered a wonderful new application of the empty water bottle to improve attention in meetings, as Bill explained:

> *Alain always used to punch me in the arm when I lost attention and drifted off into working on my laptop. And I used to return the favor. But Alain is a big fellow and a punch from him really used to hurt. One day I had just*

finished drinking a bottle of water and saw him on his BlackBerry, and before I thought about it I bounced the empty bottle off his head. It was just as effective as the punch and much less effortful for both of us. And it's catching on. Last week Martine, another colleague, launched one across the room at Francesca who was tapping away at SameTime. Now when we meet as a leadership team we always make sure we have an empty water bottle to hand.

"Good luck. You are going to need it."

I was at dinner in Italy with a career U.S. diplomat. As you might expect from someone who has being doing that job for 20 years, he was a charming, engaging, and calm individual. Until I mentioned I was writing this book.

"Meetings! Meetings have been the bane of my career. They are pointless! A complete waste of time!!" He was standing by this point and, I swear, waving a bread stick. "I say NO to all meetings now. All except one. I do one meeting a week just to remind myself why I don't go to any others!!!"

He eventually calmed down, but when I left the dinner he took me to one side. "Good luck," he said, like he was sending me into Da-Nang on a one-way mission. "You're going to need it."

He does have a point. If you really mean to change the way you meet, you are going to be messing with the culture of the business and the deep-seated habits of its employees. You're going to discover that very often the meetings are not the problem, they are a symptom of the problem. You are going to be upsetting the status quo. It could get messy.

Great meetings are a noble destination. The question is, are you prepared to do what it takes to get there? [CUE: stirring action movie soundtrack with snare drums and lone bugle. Distant at first but building to the end of this chapter.]

We're not looking for trainers (training coming as it does from the Latin to drag) but for undercover agents of change.

This isn't about moving the paper clips around. It's about setting off a meeting revolution in your business. And that's going to need meeting revolutionaries. We are looking for people who want to make a difference and understand you may need to be a little unorthodox to achieve that. It's for people who want to see a real difference in their meetings and for that effect to last. (How am I doing in enrolling you, by the way? This wouldn't be a bad way to set intent and engage people at the beginning of a meeting. Particularly if you add a warning ...)

But, before you volunteer, there's something you should know. It's a dangerous world out there in Nearly Meeting Land. The inhabitants don't like to be pushed around. They'll just push back. This is not for the shy or the unadventurous! You're going to have to be missionary, secret agent, psychologist, and aid worker rolled into one.

Before you sign up, ask yourself: are you the sort of person who could ...

> **Operate in disguise,** *changing who you appear to be to suit different meeting situations? This could also include deep deception or what we call "going native," pretending to be one of the boring people to gain their trust.*

> **Become an expert in forgery,** *quickly separating valuable meetings from counterfeit ones?*
> **Hijack** *meetings from individuals who don't know how to lead them as well as setting off the occasional full-scale mutiny to regain control when the leadership has gone to sleep?*
> **Set up revolutionary cells,** *operating under new meeting rules without permission or fear?*
> **Defuse unexploded bombs** *of emotion which lie under the surface of even polite meetings and also setting off the occasional controlled detonation?*
> **Practice biological warfare,** *releasing viruses that make your colleagues allergic to unhealthy practices and create effective new addictions to replace their current ones?*
> **Be bad.** *Nothing is going to change unless you are prepared to misbehave a little. At school you'd be punished for being a disruptive influence, here it's an entry requirement. But being bad also means not looking good. Are you willing to try something new and get it wrong? I ask because a lot of us would do anything rather than appear fallible, and even the toughest meeting revolutionaries can unravel when their ego is threatened. Mistakes are inevitable if you really commit to doing things differently. Can you handle that and learn from them?*

And, finally, could you

> **Be ruthless,** *mercilessly killing off "nearly" meetings you don't need? You'll be brutally hacking into the undergrowth of*

regular meetings choking your day. And culling the cute, furry little ad hoc meetings that look up with those puppy eyes and say, "Take me home, I won't take up much time and I'll make you feel soooo important."

If you can answer yes to these questions, then welcome to the rest of the book. Please, stand and repeat after me the motto of the Guild of Meeting Mischief Makers. "Finis ad Fastidium!"* That's "Bore No More," to you and me.

Remember, this isn't a book about boring meetings and whether you want to have them. It's a book about boring lives and whether you want to live one.

---

* Some clients do prefer the alternative Latin motto which goes: "Quaerimus Et Si Non Invenio Facimus Malum" (we go looking for trouble—and if we don't find any, we make some) but it's harder to print on a T-shirt.

1
NEARLY MEETING

The Multi-billion dollar unforced error of Business

I worked with a major UK insurance firm a few years ago. Every year eager executives would ask its CEO what his vision was for the following year. His answer was always the same: "To make one less huge mistake." He was experienced enough to know that the revenue would flow in. His concern was wasting it once it arrived. If he could tackle or prevent this year's big—and avoidable—mistake, then the revenue would really count instead of gushing away into a deep hole of the company's own making.

This chapter is about a big mistake that almost all companies are going to make this year. And the next. And the one after that. I call it *Nearly Meeting*.

How do you know if you are nearly meeting?

A nearly meeting is any meeting where the participants fail to get real value out of their coming together. They are the ones which offer a poor return on the time and effort invested—for the individuals taking part and the organizations they work for.

Nearly meetings are the ones where problems are *half* solved, the issues are *partially* understood, the right things are *almost* said. They come *that close* to being useful. If you ever stagger out of a meeting room wondering where the day went and what you did with it, you've probably been nearly meeting. You'll have *semi-resolved* problems, *almost* discussed what truly needs to be discussed and *practically* decided what to do about it.

I am reminded of Billy Crystal's magician character in William Goldman's fairytale comedy *The Princess Bride* who claims the hero isn't alive or dead, but "mostly dead." And so it is with nearly meetings. We are "mostly" meeting. And it's *completely* frustrating.

People complain about the difficulties of *virtual* meetings—as though if only people were off the phone and in a room together the problem would be solved. All nearly meetings are virtual—whether you are face to face or not. We should probably not even call them meetings at all; *missings* would be more accurate.

"Busy day, dear?"

"Murder. I've been in back-to-back missings since 7.30."

Nearly meeting is a strange no-man's-land between being separate and really connecting. I suggest it's where many of us spend the majority of our working days.

Counting the cost

Whoa. Did you just give me "the look"? It's the imperceptible tightening of the brows and lips which says, "I am a hard-nosed business person and what does this soft issue have to do with my bottom line, sonny?"

I've seen it the length and breadth of the business world, from boardroom to shop floor. And when I see it I ask clients—as I ask you now—to consider the following:

Imagine you are in a role which requires you to attend three hours of meetings a day. And let's say you'd score those meetings 70 percent effective. Let's also imagine there are 100 people like you in the company and that your average wage is, say, $100k. None of this is particularly far-fetched, you'd agree? OK, then.

You just wasted 82 days in meetings this year, costing your company a pretty significant $2m. What's more, if you were to continue at this rate for a conventional career, you'd be burning a total of nine years, six months, and three days of your working life.

This is hypothetical, but far from fantastical. Here's a real example which I put in front of the board of a major pharmaceutical company who weren't immediately convinced that ineffective meetings were having a significant effect on their business.

They'd called me in—as clients often do—to get more creativity into their working practices. People often feel this is a kind of spray-on process but quickly discover that the blocks to creativity lie in some very fundamental practicalities.

In the Pharma's case the numbers were more like 4.5 hours spent in meetings per day, 60 percent effectiveness, average fully loaded costs of $125,000 and 2500 employees. Put them through the formula and there's an eye-watering *72 million dollars* of invaluable time and cost you just poured down the drain.

By any standards that's a major mistake to be making. And to keep on making.

So yes, it's a soft issue. But with a rock hard center. It's like flying through a cloud with a nasty, big mountain hidden inside it. The implications for your financial as well as physical wellbeing can be sudden and drastic.

When I am talking to people who like to differentiate their activities in terms of "hard stuff" and "soft stuff," I like to describe the work I do particularly with meetings as "the hard-soft stuff." Soft, in that it's broadly a people issue. And hard because it's tough to fix.

When you start to really change meetings, you are tinkering with the culture of the business, and issues don't come much trickier. It's easy enough for your business to commit to culture change when you are on a blue-sky-thinking executive-retreat somewhere nice and warm. But visit the workplace a week or two later and you'll find the "nearly meeting" culture is as stuck as ever. We'll look at how to change things more effectively a little later in the book.

Nearly Meetings are a worldwide epidemic. And epidemics are something that one of my clients Thomas Breuer knows more than most about. Thomas doesn't have a golf trophy in his office.

Nor one of those toe-curling posters shot against a Hawaiian sunset saying what a real leader is made of.

Thomas Breuer, a physician and epidemiologist by training, is Head of Global Vaccine Development (GVD) at GlaxoSmithKline Vaccines. In the GVD offices there are photographs of African women and their children. They are there to remind all of them of their deadline to license a malaria vaccine and the devastating prospect on mortality in Africa if they fall behind their target. And malaria is just one area of attention. When H1N1 swine flu last threatened the world, it was on Thomas's watch. It explains why Thomas is intolerant of outdated processes and wasting time.

When Thomas took over his new role, his first act was to have multiple small informal lunches with groups across his entire staff of 1400 people.

> *What they told me again and again is that we are wasting huge time and money in meetings. The amount of money we were burning in people time in wasteful meetings was mind-blowing. I realized instead of hiring in or outsourcing there was one untapped jewel sitting in the middle of my department and that by doing meetings better I could create more time for people already in the company and who have the skills I need now.*

So, how to engage a group of medics and scientists in meetings when they'd all rather be out saving the world from rotavirus, shingles, cancer, and worse? The answer, it turned out, was to stop focusing on meeting efficiency and start thinking about meeting *health*. We set up a "meeting hospital" and for three months we took in meetings that were sick, needy, and near death and brought them back to life. Quite a few of the techniques in this book were developed in the emergency ward of the meeting hospital.

The results read like one of those "before and after" weight-loss advertisements. After three months 97 percent of participants found meetings more purposeful, clear, and engaging.

Clearly, with the right antidote and a big bucket of innovation we can tackle nearly meetings. But the question is, if they are so manifestly unhealthy, why do we keep having them?

We nearly meet because …
in a mad world it makes sense

If I worked every day in some of the companies I visit, I am certain I would be nearly meeting in a week.

When I started working with one of my clients, part of their business had a monthly six-hour conference call involving 100 people around the world. That's 72 hours a year or nearly two whole working weeks. Multiply that by the number of participants and you are looking at a collective year and a half of working life. It had better be a pretty important subject, wouldn't you think? But it wasn't. It was a business-as-usual thing. No one wants to be in that meeting. Certainly not for six hours. But no one feels that they can legitimately *not* take part. So they sit there, rolling their eyes in various locations around the world, one eye on the BlackBerry, the other on the clock, pretending to meet. In an illogical system, it's the logical response.

We dealt with this meeting in a way that I strongly recommend you try in your own company. We blew it up. And then we only put back what was absolutely needed. It turned out that the real hot topics could be best showcased in a bimonthly webforum. And the informal information sharing is now done, café style, at the end of the day every six weeks or so.

We nearly meet because ...
we have lost control of our diaries

I have come to realize that diaries are like houses. It is easy to fill them both with unwanted clutter.

In 2008 the Pearls decided to spend a couple of years living in Italy. When we rented out our house in London we put half the furniture in storage and took the rest with us to Piedmont. On our return we had only 50 percent of our original furniture and the house felt—absolutely fine! Or to put it another way, we had been living with twice as much stuff as we needed but hadn't noticed because we had got so used to all the clutter around us, we'd stopped seeing it. So, now take a look at your diary and all the meetings in it. Which half needs to go into storage? There will be two kinds of meetings cluttering up your day: *Standing* meetings and *Ad Hoc* ones.

Standing meetings are the regular ones which are fixed (daily, weekly, monthly, quarterly) at the beginning of the year and/or project. They are like the furniture, fixtures, and fittings. You don't necessarily know who gave them to you or why they are there, but they have been around so long you have ceased to notice them; they have become the background to your life. The rest are Ad Hoc meetings. They appear unexpectedly in response to a situation, problem or request. I think of these as impulse buys that you see at the weekend and "must have," or mail—including junk mail—that arrives in your letterbox clamoring for your attention.

The rules for de-cluttering a house or diary are very similar. You need a brutal cull of the unwanted contents you have accumulated and a severely selective, No Junk, entry policy to prevent any new garbage crossing the threshold.

We nearly meet because …
it's an attractive alternative to real work

Steve, a prominent LA tax and business advisor, takes client service seriously. And so he should. His starry clients are the sort of people who expect him to be on call 24/7.

In case you were thinking your senior people are capriciously demanding, you should spend a day or two in the performing arts where Stars can be really Starry. One tale I know to be true from my time in the opera world is that of a sumptuously gifted but notoriously high-maintenance operatic soprano who was feeling a little warm in the back of her limo while driving through Manhattan. Too grand to lean forward and ask the driver to turn up the air-conditioning, she picked up the limo phone, called her agent in Los Angeles, who then called the driver in New York with the message.

NEARLY MEETING

Steve talks of his earlier career in a large corporate practice where he was expected to attend a daily meeting at 11.00 known (I kid you not) as the Donut Meeting because there was nothing much else to talk about. "I was an outlier," he admits.

> *I was one of the few people who thought that if you are in a service company that the real priority was to, well, serve clients. I felt that instead of sitting around shooting the breeze there might be things that the client would actually want you to do, things you were, er, paid to do. So I used to excuse myself from the Donut meetings and go to talk to some clients. Actually pick up the phone and speak to them. It seemed to me that most of the others were actually scared of doing that. You'd ask them if they had called client A and they'd answer yes. "When?" Three weeks ago. "And since then?" Well, they'd been busy in meetings.*
>
> *Clients don't want to hear you are in meetings. They want to hear you on the other end of the phone. It's not great telling billionaire clients bad news, but I find it's always better than hiding away. Instead of holding a Donut meeting, I would go and talk to a few people and get the job done.*

Steve has nicely summed up one of the key messages of this book. Instead of holding wasteful meetings, get out there and start having the real meetings and conversations that really matter.

Or, as the T-shirt would say: Fewer Meetings—More Meeting.

We nearly meet because ... technology* makes it so easy

It's 10.58 on the bustling concourse of a London train station. Suddenly a granny throws down her walking stick and starts jiving. All over the station people join her. They dance in concentration and in silence, perfectly synchronized by the music they hear on their iPod headphones. Exactly two minutes 11 seconds later the dance stops as magically as it started and the participants melt away.

The Flash Mob that has just happened is a great illustration of how technology helps us nearly meet. None of this would have been possible without the internet. The participants convened online, practiced their dance at home via web cams, texted each other where and when to meet. Everything has been prepared and performed at arm's length. That's its beauty and irony. It's less entertainment and more a shared personal experience for those in the know. A silent dance, an un-performance by non-performers. A crowd of people dancing alone is so very 21st-century. And a perfect illustration of how technology loves us to nearly meet.

---

*As US computer pioneer Alan Kay pointed out, "technology" is a name we give to any technical advance invented after we were born. For my parents' generation, the color television came under the heading of technology. Not for mine. Television was as normal as plumbing. For us it's laptops and wifi. Who knows what our kids will think of and see as technology? Looking back, though, there must have been a time when a table with four legs was the most advanced, jaw-dropping meeting technology on the planet. I'd like to have been there to see that.

I really admire people who have embraced the nearly meeting medium with creative flair. People like Eric Whiteacre who have created amazing online choirs, or StreetWars, who galvanize whole towns into staging water pistol ambushes through social media.

That said, I am doubtful about whether all this supposed digital connectivity has actually brought us closer as human beings.

I met a London cabbie the other day. He was a chatty guy but was looking subdued. "Just had a lady in my cab and asked her, 'How are you today?' She gave me a filthy look and shouted, 'I am married, you know,' as though fending off an attack." Apparently this is happening to him once a week. A most basic human exchange is taken as a threat of violence.

America, the most netted-up nation on earth, is increasingly the land of the loner. In his book *Bowling Alone*, Harvard professor Robert Putnam shows how Americans have become increasingly disconnected. Family dinners have apparently dropped by 43 percent in 25 years; people are 35 percent less likely to have friends over to their houses; and bowling alleys across the country are increasingly used by individuals competing against themselves.

Thanks to Twitter, Facebook, and LinkedIn we are accruing vast numbers of "friends" we'll never meet. In many cases live meeting is actively discouraged. Even my eight-year-old son knows not to show his face on screen and to use a coded name when talking to his mates in Seattle or Brazil about the latest Lego craze.

It's all very flattering to have a huge network, but drain the digital bath of drive-by acquaintances and people trying to sell you something, and how many real relationships do you find?

The other day someone I haven't seen for 20 years—and barely knew back then—waved to me at a concert and wished me Happy Birthday. How the hell did she know? Apparently my Wall told her. Walls don't just have ears any more. They have mouths. I didn't feel flattered. I felt stalked.

Clearly there is a dissonance between the media we have available to connect with others and our success in using them.

Nowhere does technology facilitate nearly meeting better than our busy, busy businesses. Co-workers email each other rather than look around the computer screen and talk. Meeting tables come ready plumbed for laptops, so face time and screen time inevitably compete.

I am looking forward to the time when someone recommends the face-to-face meeting as a wild new innovation. I suspect it's not far away. Especially when people are making such a fuss about new technologies which are—drum roll—in 3D. Our lives are in 3D, if only you'd rip your eyes away from your 2D screen long enough to notice that!

I'm struck by how we are using all sorts of very tactile, kinetic verbs—ping, prod, tweet, twang—to describe interactions that are totally disembodied. How funny that we talk about using technology to stay in *touch* when there's no touching at all. OK, I give my Apple the occasional loving stroke, but ...

If I am sounding Luddite, I don't mean to. Technology enables businesses to cut down on the time and cost involved in physically bringing their people together. And let's not forget, this is also in the interests of the planet, minimizing the carbon carnage of those unnecessary international flights.

But virtual meetings are—as their name plainly advertises—not real. They encourage us to almost, just about, *nearly* meet. It's a real challenge to make and keep real human connection with disembodied voices or truncated torsos across continents and time zones. We'll look later in the book at how to make the best of the medium and "create intimacy at a distance."

Bottom line: just because technology *can* connect us, it doesn't mean we *do* really connect.

A colleague told me a poignant story about a friend of his, a top-flight corporate lawyer who spends her time jetting around the world, constantly in touch with clients on one of her two BlackBerries by text, BMS, email, and MMS. Recently, on a fevered dash from one meeting to another, she flipped her car and was nearly killed. Staggering out of the wreckage and just glad to be alive, she reached for her phone to tell her loved ones that she was all right and realized she had no one to call.

The ability to really connect is natural, but requires practice or it withers, with predictably negative effects on both our business and personal lives.

We nearly meet because ... that's what we want to do

Let's face it, other people are hard work. They have this annoying habit of not agreeing with us. They have their own ideas and agendas. They don't, for some reason, think we are always marvelous. They are complex, demanding and just plain tiring.

Why would we want to meet them? Better by far to *pretend* to meet. Nod but don't hear. Smile but don't mean it. Keep "them" on the outside and save your energy.

When I am not in London—or on a plane—I spend as much time as I can in rural Italy. As a lifelong city dweller I am acutely aware of how few people you see on a normal day in the north Italian countryside. The scarcity of the people seems to put them into high relief. You notice them. They notice you. Your eyes meet. You raise your hand. You briefly discuss the ripeness of the tomatoes, the likelihood of rain, the latest aches and pains and whether Juventus are likely to scrape through this season without pouring shame on the team/the region/the nation. It is the sort of setting which encourages connections with others. London is another story. As I take the plane, taxi, or tube back into the center of the metropolis, I feel my mind becoming overwhelmed by potential connection. There are just too many people. I start to screen them out, like the iris of your eye shutting down to protect you from a blast of bright sunlight. Within minutes I am in a bubble where I can walk through a crowd of people on Oxford Street and see—no one.

This ability of the mind to filter out information is a key to our development as a species—and our survival as modern humans. The ability selectively to screen out background sounds so we hear what is being said to us is key to our communication. It is similarly crucial to our survival that we can separate the features of a landscape we don't need to know about (the green stuff) from the things we might need to know about (like a saber-toothed tiger).

There is growing concern at the connection between the use of digital music players and fatal accidents. The London authorities have started talking about "iPod zombies" and San Francisco has spent millions on a media blitz warning against the screening-out effect of earphones. "Do you want Beethoven to be the last thing you hear?" one lugubrious ad asks the city's joggers.

We nearly meet because …
we confuse efficient and effective

As the doyen of management consultants Peter Drucker once said, "Efficiency is doing things right; effectiveness is doing the right things." Many companies are focusing on making their meetings more efficient. That doesn't mean they are any more effective.

I have a friend who is a world-class management consultant. I'll call him Ron—not his real name—for the sake of discretion and to prevent his clients taking out a contract on me. He has a great example of a client who has become exquisitely efficient and wildly ineffective at the same time. It's all to do with paper. The client generates hundreds of thousands of sheets of contracts and agreements at each of their branches every week. The company has had to become supremely talented at moving all this paper around as well as storing and retrieving it. They have invested in ergonomically designed paper-carrying equipment (I think this means strong suitcases), transportation systems, and document logging. They were thrilled with themselves until Ron asked the unasked question: "Why do you need all this paper?" They were ready for this. "Because the regulator requires that we get our customers' signature." Ron pressed on: "Yes, but why does that signature have to be on paper?" he asked, no doubt making a lifelong enemy of the Logistics Director. In this digital age there are many legally acceptable forms of signature, of which a mark on paper is only one. There's a tick on a form, a digitally scanned signature, a thumbprint, even the iris in your eye. Ron's point was that while the paper is being dealt with efficiently, the more effective course of action would be to invest a tiny fraction of the time, energy, and money into talking with the regulator and finding a paperless solution. Efficient, yes. Effective, no!

I have seen efficient meetings—meticulously planned, immaculately laid out and run perfectly to time—that had no positive *effect* whatever. (We'll look a little later in the book at how to redesign meetings so that they are both.) These are classic "nearly meetings." And they are going to be happening all over the world today and every day. The people are present, or appear to be; the room or the call/video conference suite is booked, the agenda prepared, and yet no connection in a true sense actually happens.

We nearly meet because ... we forget there's an alternative

Finally, the most pervasive reason of all, we nearly meet so much because we don't realize, remember, or believe we can *really* meet.

I am reminded of a leadership programme we were involved in delivering to the top echelons of a major European financial services company. It was held in a spectacular castle on the outskirts of Paris. At the end of our three days together the participants were talking about what they had gotten out of the experience. One man was asked what he had learned. I knew that this self-confessed "numbers guy" was earmarked for great things, but he looked terribly awkward as he said his piece.

"Every Monday I have a meeting with the people who report to me and I usually just like to get on with it. I don't see any need to talk to them about themselves, how they are or what they're up to. I am a doer and I see this kind of thing as a waste of time. What I didn't realize until now, though, was that there was a real person sitting opposite me."

He then sat down, looking somewhat apologetic and puzzled by an insight that was at once so mundane and yet so far-reaching—not just for his career but beyond.

I think this client spoke for all of us who crash through the day, intent on getting things done, and forgetting to connect with the people around us. We forget they are people, not just "functions."

It's because of stories like this that I've become curious about meetings. We go into meetings disconnected not only from others but also from our own thoughts, feelings, bodies, and our true nature.

Realizing that nearly meeting is mostly what you are doing is a great first step to start really meeting.

The True Cost of Nearly Meeting

Nearly meeting is exacting a huge cost not just on us and our businesses but on our planet.

Great meetings can save the world. Bad ones can really harm it. I can think of no better opportunity of a world-sized missed opportunity than the 2009 United Nations Climate Change Conference in Copenhagen. I wasn't there, but I've heard from friends who were that it was a fiasco. A nearly meeting on an epic scale. With epic consequences.

The problems started even before you got into the conference venue. Thanks to inadequate—or willfully negligent—planning, entry lines stretched for hundreds of yards and required ticket holders to stand in the open air, sometimes for several hours, in polar conditions, without the comfort of heating, refreshments, or even a coffee. Coffee sellers wanted to set up concessions but were not allowed to. It was as though the Danes, normally quite welcoming folk, wanted to discourage people from attending.

There wasn't even a fast-track entrance for VIPs. Ashok Khosla, Chairman of the New Delhi-based social enterprise, Development Alternatives, who is also the current President of the International Union for the Conservation of Nature (IUCN) found himself grid-locked in a non-moving mass of humanity and was clearly about to miss his speaking slot. If you know sustainable development, you know of Ashok. He's been described by the United Nations Environment Programme as "a legend in the realm of sustainable development, and an individual who personifies the hopes and dreams of billions trapped in the indignity of acute deprivation." This didn't impress the slab-faced security guards. He only managed to get to the front of the line by distracting one of them by making a comment on her guard-dog's condition.

Once inside (and many people gave up before they ever managed to enter), the problems were worse. The unlovely venue, wonderfully misnamed as the Bella Centre, seemed custom-designed to make you lose your way—a maze of small committee rooms and misleading signs.

There is a well-known YouTube film of the then British Prime Minister, Gordon Brown, sweeping confidently into what he thinks is a meeting room only to find himself in a cupboard. President Obama likewise had to go on a peek-a-boo treasure hunt through the corridors to find that his meeting with the Chinese delegation was already underway without him.

The Chinese premier was in the building (like Elvis) but famously refused to meet his U.S. counterpart face to face. Brinksmanship? Diplomatic theater? Or an unwillingness to have a real meeting?

Guardian journalist Mark Lynas was in no doubt: "The Chinese premier, Wen Jinbao, did not deign to attend the meetings personally, instead sending a second-tier official in the country's foreign ministry to sit opposite Obama himself. The diplomatic snub was obvious and brutal, as was the practical implication: several times during the session, the world's most powerful heads of state were forced to wait around as the Chinese delegate went off to make telephone calls to his 'superiors'."

This was pure power politics—*nearly meeting* at its most blatant. Clearly at a meeting like this, each nation will have its own agenda to pursue. In some cases, minimizing perceived threats to their economic growth; in others, like the Maldives, literally keeping their heads above rising seawater.

This need not have been a problem, had the participants really wanted to use this meeting to make the world a cleaner and safer place. But they did not. China and others clearly had no intention of playing anything but their own game. And as we are going to see a little later, intention is all.

The power plays of Copenhagen set the precedent for COP 17 in Durban in 2011, where we were treated to the unedifying sight of Saudi Arabia's oil sheikhs holding the meeting—and the world—to ransom by insisting that they be compensated for losses they would suffer if the world stopped burning fossil fuels. As the *Economist* reported:

> *Most of the scores of diplomats present were appalled. Not least those from small island nations, like Kiribati and Tuvalu, which are likely to disappear beneath the rising seas long before the Saudis have drained their last well. But it mattered naught ... After a fraught few hours of bickering, the Saudis got their wretched commitment.*

That's nearly meeting. In place of collaboration there is bargaining. An opportunity for joint action descends into a clash of competing ideologies. I was in a meeting recently where Trevor Manuel, formerly Nelson Mandela's finance minister and currently the head of South Africa's Planning Commission, summed up the limits of this approach. "Ideology means you know the answer before you hear the question." Instead of real conversation you get ping-pong rallies of pre-prepared attitudes and opinion.

The COP events are a particularly high-stakes unforced error. But I would suggest that every *nearly meeting* we hold goes some way to destroying value in our world.

Nearly meetings are not just unproductive, they are counter-productive because they undermine our trust in the power of really meeting.

And really meeting can change the world ...

2
REALLY MEETING

One of the realest "real meetings" I ever attended was held by a teacher and inspiration of mine, the enigmatic and bear-like Michael Breen. Pioneer of Neuro-Linguistic Programming (NLP) and a great business consultant, Michael is not a man of many words but you had better listen up, because the ones he uses matter.

Michael walked to the front of the room, looked at us with a smile and simply asked: "Any Questions?"

That was it. As it happened, there were a load of questions and the meeting was a fascinating one. Two hours shot by in a flash. But if there hadn't been a question, Michael wouldn't have continued. It would have been the shortest meeting on record. But it would have been real.

I am tempted to treat this chapter the same way. Having comprehensively savaged, mocked, and character-assassinated all those "nearly meetings," I am hoping that the value of really meeting is self-evident. And leave it at that.

However ...

I have been working in business long enough to know that there *will* be questions. And they are going to come at you thick and fast when you start changing meetings.

To you it's obvious that really meeting your fellow humans in an effective, authentic, and elegant way will generate more value in your company, improve relationships with colleagues and customers, resolve conflicts at home, at work and in the world. You think it's unarguable that genuine rather than fake meetings lead to better decisions, clearer actions, more interesting products and services.

You'd think. However, the questions and challenges will come. People don't like mediocrity, but it is amazing how hard they will argue for it when you offer a change.

One person you are going to bump into on your travels is the Rolex Warrior. He (for it usually is a he) will walk—or rather weave—up to you in the bar at some point, wearing a striped shirt that makes your eyes strobe. And he's going to ask you, point-blank: "What's the point of this really meeting stuff?"

It's a rhetorical question. He means, "There is no point. Business is the way it is. It may be mediocre, but there's no way things are going to change."

I look him coolly in the eye. "The value of really meeting? Ask your wife. Sorry, ex-wife." That's in my fantasy anyway, where I am played by a bullet-dodging, black-coated Keanu Reeves. Back in real life, I'm gripping my beer with a polite smile and I probably point out that:

Really Meeting makes us Smarter

Once a month I walk out onto a theater stage in London's West End to sing an opera I have never learned, with music I have never heard, characters that are completely new and no idea of where the story starts or ends. It's like that recurrent nightmare people have about appearing naked in public with no script, combined with the pathological fear others have about having to sing in front of an audience.

I should say I am not alone, but part of a group of fellow thrill-seekers who make up the world's only improvising opera company, Impropera (www.impropera.co.uk).

It's never comfortable, but what makes it hugely valuable every time is to experience what a group of people can collectively invent when they are put under real pressure.

In the improv world it is called "Group Mind," the capacity of several minds to think "as one." When the show is good we each have a feeling that someone else came up with the good ideas. It's the glue that holds together TV improv shows like *Whose Line Is It Anyway?* And I suggest it's one of the key components of real meetings.

When you are really meeting, people don't hang on to their own ideas but build on each others'. Instead of the plague of "buts" that stifle nearly meetings and stop the creative process flowing, a real meeting is full of "yesses" as the participants accept what is emerging and build on it. It's business jazz.

Ron the Consultant sounds more like a jazz improviser than a business professional when he says, "A great meeting is where you turn up with 20 pages but use none of them. Instead you get up, gather round the flipchart and together you deal with what needs to be done."

There's a stark contrast with the "every person for themselves" character of the nearly meeting, as Pharma senior executive Thomas Breuer explains:

> *It's a fundamental problem when you have a series of monologues happening. It's so tempting just to leap in with your own idea. My colleagues and I have now trained ourselves to say "I paid a lot of attention to what you said—now let me build on this and give my view." You create much higher value when you really concentrate on what the previous person said, rather than go 180 degrees with a completely disconnected idea. We now make a conscious effort to create something of higher value by joining the dots. When we do this the output of the meeting multiplies.*

When you are in flow like this, your individuality seems to be replaced by a group identity. The ideas don't originate from the individuals but emerge in the space between them.

It's as if you are individual fingers but on the same hand. You hear sportspeople talk about this heightened team feeling. Likewise, soldiers working with comrades under testing conditions. While it's crazy to think of the thumb and finger competing with each other, that is effectively what is happening when we nearly meet.

If you look down on meetings from an imaginary bird's-eye viewpoint—and I recommend this perspective whenever you get stuck—participants look less like human beings and more like components of a larger network. I think of many radio telescopes combining to create an array of receivers that's far more sensitive than a single unit. Seen from this eye-in-the-sky angle, a meeting isn't really generating ideas, it's amplifying the ones it picks up from "out there."

"Out there" is where the customer is, where the business is really taking place, where the future is forming and true innovation lurks. Addicts of the inward-looking process meeting would do well to "turn the dish" outwards, because that is where the value is usually to be found.

Another word for this experience of flow is "ensemble," a performing arts term—from the French word meaning "together"—for a group of virtuosos who agree to play, write and perform together. Though the myth of the lone genius is widely promoted in the arts world, the majority of great work is done by ensembles really meeting and creating together.

Really Meeting Creates Clarity

One of the functions of really meeting is that we leave clearer than when we arrived.

I think clarity is a Holy Grail of business. Something that people want but requires a real quest to find. Clarity is hard to achieve by yourself. If you listen, your mind is a constant swirl of signals. When the time comes to be clear, your mind hasn't made up its mind.

"How can I know what I think till I see what I say?" as the little girl asked. Real Meetings help us get clearer, collectively, than we could do individually.

A common criticism of religion is that it requires you to accept dogma in an unthinking way. I am not particularly religious, but coming from a Jewish background I can't help noticing how un-accepting Jews seem to be when they want to get clear. The process is dynamic, argumentative, and usually very noisy. Scholars studying the Talmud traditionally sit opposite each other on specially constructed tables and basically argue with each other about the meaning of every word and phrase. I don't know if this explains why there are so many Jewish lawyers, but I think I understand why our family meals were so noisy when I was growing up.

When we really meet, truths aren't dispensed but are hammered out across a table. The sacred texts are not accepted in a pre-digested, face-value way but only gather meaning through the to and fro of discussion. You only get clear when you get collective ...

Really Meeting is Inclusive

There was a great moment in music history, in around 1300, when church choirs stopped chanting in unison and burst into glorious "polyphony," where lots of diverse voices singing different lines weave together into a rich, complex harmony.

Really meeting is like that. It operates in quadrasonic surround sound. It enables all voices to be heard ... even the quiet ones.

As Thomas Breuer explains, it can be a challenge, but it's worth the effort:

> *When you put people together from very different fields and hierarchy levels you have to spend time to make sure that everyone really speaks up and each individual contribution is recognized. Hierarchy in innovative meetings is counterproductive. I imagine it's a bit like how an orchestral conductor has to pay equal attention to the entire brass section and the solo piccolo.*
>
> *If I have a lot of people sitting around me who are senior management peers, then fine. But if you have physicians, statisticians or analysts responsible for the data management of a project it is essential to encourage them to speak up and bring them up to a level where they can contribute.*
>
> *I find that these people often have crucial insights to offer that raise the conversation or bring it down to earth. If they don't speak up and instead leave the meeting thinking "Too bad," we are losing value.*
>
> *Everyone is used to the cliché there are no stupid questions, but to create an atmosphere where this is really the case requires a lot from the person running the meeting. Everyone has to know there will be no punishment for so-called "dumb" suggestions. The creation of a common understanding, culture, platform is important. Management has to create a common language, a license to operate, so that people dare to speak up.*

I remember a safety meeting when the imminent swine flu pandemic and the expected distribution of tens of millions of vaccine doses was going to result in an exponential growth of safety events; 20 to 25 times more than the safety department could normally handle. We were starting to think about this. Who else can rapidly join the safety team? Can we get additional resources from other functions in- or outside the company? Then all of a sudden one guy spoke up. He is not very senior but he really knows our operation. He's what I call a quiet voice. "You know," he said, "resource is only one way to approach this. Another way is to look at our processes and take fat out of the system. Why don't we engage with governmental agencies and explore ways to stagger reporting on products which have been in the market for 15 to 20 years?"

This one comment triggered an avalanche of new ideas. That's what I mean by a really inclusive meeting.

Really Meeting allows Real Conversations to happen

"You don't really want to have a war, do you, your Highness?"

It's not a phrase that you or I might use too often. But it's the sort of conversational gambit you might need at your fingertips if you happen to be the head of a global NGO like Oxfam. Dame Barbara Stocking is a fan of really meeting. She has to be when dealing with potentially explosive international situations.

There is a head of state I can think of who thinks the world is against him. He is constantly about to go to war with a neighboring state. So recently I got on a plane. The fact that I took the trouble to go out there and visit him was already an important step. Sometimes just showing up is the key. We had a very human discussion and in the middle of it I just asked him point-blank if he really intended to go to war. After quite a pause he replied. "No, I don't want to do that."

Nearly meeting skirts the dangerous issues. When you are really meeting, people say what they mean, mean what they say, and the conversations that need to happen take place.

This is a great example of what I call "taking the gorilla off the fridge." Essentially, if there is a subject which should be talked about but isn't, you severely compromise the quality of your meeting. Imagine having a gorilla on your fridge while you are having Sunday dinner. Everyone is carrying on as normal, but everyone knows things are far from OK. Some people call this having "an elephant in the room." Different animal, equally debilitating effect. My advice is to refer to the un-talked-about beast right from the start. When you set up a meeting you can include a phrase like "I know some of you are thinking X ..." or "If I were in your shoes, I know I'd be wondering about Y."

You don't have to go into detail, but just mentioning the unmentionable eases tension and creates the conditions where a real meeting can occur.

Thomas Breuer points to two other key factors when he talks about the importance of "a common language" and "a license to operate" in encouraging real conversations to happen. The in-depth work we have done with him and his organization showed how important it is that everyone has a common understanding of what a real conversation means and that they know they are mandated to have them with colleagues irrespective of their level in the hierarchy. Once you have achieved these two things, real conversations start to propagate through an organization like a healthy "virus." "Let's have a real conversation" becomes a common phrase that's no more threatening than "Let's have a coffee." You've turned what was an exotic and rather threatening idea into a common currency.

Very few large organizations have really done that groundwork. So it's often up to individuals—up to you—to start the ball rolling. As we'll see later in the book, there are many reasons we might choose to back off from and miss the opportunity for really meeting. It requires some confidence in yourself and a real trust in the value of Real Conversation.

"It took a bit of nerve to ask him the war question" admits Dame Barbara, and she is, I can assure you, no wallflower. "But it was worth it to get the subject on the table. I really do believe that all people are equal, so at one level, I don't care."

What touches me about the story is that once you create human connection, really meeting another human being, anything is possible.

Really Meeting is Three-Dimensional

Looking at the modern working environment I can't help thinking we human beings have designed a world we weren't really designed for. A few centuries of listening to the head and more or less ignoring the wisdom of the body have produced a world that makes sense to the head but bewilders the noble physical being that's hiding beneath our business suits.

"And here," they say proudly when they show you around their offices for the first time, "is the meeting room." There is the big, important-looking table, surrounded by those heavy, expensive chairs. And a bowl of mints. To the human animal inside us, that room is clearly a place of punishment, not work.

Really meeting recognizes that humans are three-dimensional beings designed to move as well as think. If you look through a window at a real meeting, you'll see movement. Some people are gesticulating, making shapes in the air to communicate the shapes in their minds. Some people are pacing the room. Others have their feet on the table with their eyes closed and are rubbing their temples.

If a real meeting gets "stuck," the participants know that a bit of physical movement can unstick it. You take a break, a short walk, have a stretch, call a time-out. If you need more inspiration, you literally get some fresh air; because the lithe, versatile physical being that we once were, remembers that when you refill your lungs you also recharge your mind.

Real meetings are three-dimensional because we are, too.

Really Meeting is the new Work

I like to ask business audiences to look at their fingernails. Very few of them have coal dust, soil, or heavy machine oil underneath them. In general, business life doesn't include the physical labor of clawing commodities out of the earth, harvesting by hand, or grappling with heavy machinery.

We are moving into a post-industrial age where knowledge and ideas are the assets. Meetings are where these assets are formed and traded. They are to our times what the steam hammer, forge, and mill were to the Industrial Age.

Meetings are where value is created—or lost. When people complain that meetings are getting in the way of their work, you might want to point out that, increasingly, meetings *are* the work.

Information, ideas, concepts are the new commodities. Intellectual property is as valuable as bricks and mortar. The meeting is the modern mine ...

Great businesses like Marks *and* Spencer, Procter *and* Gamble, Dolce *and* Gabbana, Ben *and* Jerry remind us that commerce stems from the meeting of two or more minds. The word Company (from the Old French for companions) appears in the names of millions of enterprises—another reminder that value is generated where and when people meet.

Sole proprietors are rarely that. They operate as small gatherings of friends and families. More and more people are self-employed, but that doesn't mean people are working alone. As Tom Ball, CEO of the London-based "co-working" venture Neardesk, explains:

> *About 13 percent of the U.K. workforce now works from home for part, if not all, of the week. For many it's an attractive alternative to the traditional commute-to-the-office life. However, people often discover that sitting at*

home quickly becomes boring and lonely. They can rent small offices, but they're still alone. For this reason we are seeing a real growth in what we call co-working, where individuals gather in "business hubs" so they can get the benefits of being "in company" without the commuting life and all the stress that comes with it. They bump into people, have stimulating conversations, trip over business opportunities they would otherwise have missed. They get the best of both worlds. I think in a few years belonging to a business club or hub—being part of this new kind of self-creating business community—will be as common as gym membership.

Mac or Mozzarella? A question of quality

Really meeting helps us solve the problems we have and avoid bigger ones in future. It's an engine of enterprise, past and future. It's how we do deals, build things, make stuff happen. It makes us smarter than we can ever be by ourselves, helping us create value, better understand our world, lead richer lives and have better relationships. It's how we can, hopefully, create common ground, resolve conflict, and prevent ourselves from boiling our planet or blowing ourselves into oblivion.

But will knowing this change things?

I think the ultimate argument for real meetings—the choice between genuine and fake—is about the quality of the lives we want to lead.

They say the quality of your life reflects what you are prepared to tolerate. If you can put up with lousy, endless meetings then you are certain to get more of them. I recommend clients become intolerant of "nearly meeting." Allergies are trendy these days. Everyone has one. So why not become allergic, as an entire organization, to junk meetings? The thing about allergies (to gluten, peanuts, the fabric inside airline pillows) is that your body will let you know—in no uncertain terms— when any of that unhealthy stuff comes near. If we sneezed or broke out in a rash when someone suggested "nearly" meeting, we'd quickly train ourselves to seek out "really meeting" instead.

When McDonalds caused uproar by moving into the southern Italian town of Altamura in Apulia in 2001, local baker Luigi Digesu decided to take a stand. Five years later the juggernaut food chain admitted defeat and withdrew. They weren't beaten back by protest, but by quality. Luigi had not set out to force McDonald's to close down in any "bellicose spirit." He had merely offered the 65,000 residents tasty panini filled with local ingredients like mortadella, mozzarella, basil, and chopped tomatoes, which they had overwhelmingly preferred to hamburgers and chicken nuggets. "It is a question of free choice," concluded the baker.

When you try to change meetings in your company you may well face the same sort of arguments that Luigi and his slow-food companions faced. "Poor quality is cheaper" … "It's not ideal but it'll do" … "There isn't enough quality to go around" … "We're too busy to make the change" … "A whole industry is set up for low quality, high volume. High quality would be nice, but it's not practical."

The answer, as it was for Luigi, is to make your meetings so mouthwatering and wholesome that those unhealthy nearly meetings don't stand a chance.

And how do you create meetings "to die for," not die from? Read on!

3

THE ANATOMY OF MEETINGS

"Is there any point to which you would wish to draw my
attention?"

"To the curious incident of the dog in the night-time."

"The dog did nothing in the night-time."

"That was the curious incident," remarked Sherlock Holmes.

Sir Arthur Conan Doyle: *Silver Blaze*

This section is about giving you a map of what's really happening
in meetings, not just on the surface but behind the scenes and
beneath the waterline. With this insider knowledge of meetings
you can design them better, and next time things start going awry
you'll know where the problem is and how to fix it.

Fix is probably the wrong word, by the way. If this laptop goes
wrong I can fix it. Actually Carlo or Guy can fix it—I can just curse

at it. You can fix objects, but people aren't objects. They are complex living organisms. And when they get together in meetings, things get even more complex.

Some aspects of meetings are clear to see and hear. Others are invisible and have to be sensed. To really understand meetings you need to keep track not only of what is happening but also, like Sherlock Holmes noting the dog that *didn't bark*, what isn't happening and should be.

Meetings don't come with a manual and can't be "fixed" like a leaking pipe or wobbly shelf. I mention this because, in these mechanistic times, we tend to forget.

It's a material world we live in, particularly the business world. Just look at the language businesses use to flat-pack lots of messy human stuff into neat-sounding concepts like "process" and "mechanism," "resource" and "management." It's like linguistic IKEA. When we tidy up our language the world seems so much more more ordered and easy to handle.

Businesses also like to make uncomfortably invisible things reassuringly physical. So, organizations are described as if they were solid objects, with a top and a bottom, breadth and depth. There's a *back* office and a *front* line, *internal* zones and *external* ones. There's even a temperature gauge, with burning platforms and perma-frost. Metaphors are very useful. They help us make the abstract more real or "put a tea-cup handle on a cloud," as someone deliciously described them. Using this metaphorical language about business can be very helpful provided we remember that organizations are not machines, people are not resources, and meetings, unlike wobbly shelves, cannot be fixed with a tool.

If you are a tool-lover, I offer these two pieces of advice.

Giving people a tool is no guarantee they'll use it.

I know businesses that have more tools than a giant hardware store but where no one ever picks them up.

Don't give people a more powerful tool than they can handle. They could take their leg off.

I am thinking, for example, of the people I have seen who have just discovered MBTI (Myers-Briggs Type Indicator—a psychometric test) or some other personality typing "toolkit." Like any born-again convert they'll stop you in the corridor with that faraway look to ask if you are "a T or a J, a Red or a Yellow, a Summer or a Winter." I did once know a performance coach who became a little zealous about "appreciative enquiry." When his wife phoned from a distant airport to say she had missed her plane and was stranded there with their one-year-old daughter, his reaction was to ask, "And what do you learn from that?" Like I said, you could lose a leg. Or worse.

When I tried to buy a chainsaw from my local Italian hardware store, the owner looked me carefully up and down. Clearly English. Clearly no idea about the havoc a "moto-sega" can inflict. He thrust some chain-mail reinforced trousers across the counter and made it clear he wouldn't sell me a power tool without the power protection. It was a case of "No chain-mail? No chainsaw."

So, people are not objects. And meetings are not collections of objects. Which is why I want you to start thinking of meetings not as *things* at all but as *living beings*. Clients often find that a strange idea at first—especially given how inert many of their meetings are. But it's a powerful one.

When we think of a meeting as "alive":

› *we're less surprised by its complexity*
› *we start looking at it more holistically*
› *we're more respectful of it—it's not a disposable commodity*
› *we notice it repays our efforts when we take care of its vitality, rather than purely its efficiency*
› *we realize that shutting it in an airless, windowless concrete box in a hotel basement, sorry Business Suite, may not be the best idea*
› *we know it will have its good and bad days, just like us*

Treat it as another metaphor if you like. For me, after many years of doing this work, it's a reality. If I am observing a six-person meeting I'll see seven actual participants: the six people present *plus the meeting itself.*

If something goes wrong, I ask people not to blame each other, but to look up and pay attention to what the meeting needs. Is it getting over-heated or over-pressured? Is the meeting running out of energy? Does it need a break? With very little practice this exercise greatly increases your awareness of what's really needed in a meeting, moment to moment.

So, from here onwards, I want you/us to think of a meeting as a living being. And that we are not *fixing* them but keeping them healthy and vitally *alive*.

Unfortunately, living beings don't come with instructions. And if we want our meetings to function well, we do need a way to keep track of all that's happening—the obvious and not so obvious, the dogs that bark and those that don't. Fortunately, I found one. In Peru.

I was in Lima with my circus-cum-opera company (long story) and wasn't looking for a multi-dimensional meeting map. I was there to sing, eat gerbil, and get altitude sickness. One morning, our director David handed me a book he'd found on a shelf at his hotel. Please forgive the cliché, but Ken Wilber's *A Brief History of Everything* is genuinely a life-changing book. At least it was for me.

I urge you to read it if you have ever had the feeling that everything is connected but you are not sure how. The Integral approach (www.integralinstitute.org) that Wilber has pioneered is now being used the world over to help us think, act, govern, work, and live in much more holistic, healthy ways. Back then, what struck me was how it could help us have great meetings.

At the heart of the book is a simple diagram. The really great ones are simple. It's a two-by-two matrix (aren't they always?) dreamed up by the novelist and science writer Arthur Koestler, who called it a "holon."

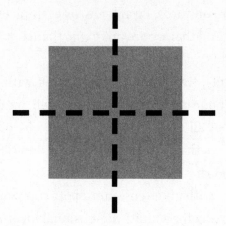

What this diagram reminds us is that everything in the universe (including meetings) has an outside and an inside ...

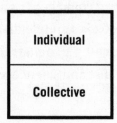

Meanwhile it is a "thing" in itself and is also a part of one or more groups:

<table>
<tr><td>Individual</td></tr>
<tr><td>Collective</td></tr>
</table>

Combine them and you get four domains, which Wilber calls:

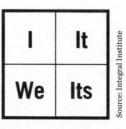

Source: Integral Institute

Think about yourself as you sit reading this book. You have a physical form—an outside made of flesh, bone and muscle, with limbs you can move and toes you can wiggle. That's the right-hand side of the diagram.

To move to the left-hand side, close your eyes for a moment and become aware of what's simultaneously happening in the interior you. Here you are a continuous ferment of thoughts, feeling, beliefs, pictures, senses.

To experience the top half, concentrate on all the aspects that make you unique and different from everyone else—the unique, separate you. And finally, as individual as you are, consider how many groups or "clubs" you are part of: human race, family, company, people with the same name/star sign/language/height. You've moved into the bottom, collective half of the Holon.

Taken together, it's a map of all we are experiencing moment to moment. In life. At work. And in meetings.

A meeting has an outside (where things are said and done) and an inside (what is going on beneath the surface—the world of beliefs, politics, emotions, hidden agendas ...). It is made up of individuals—each with their identity and role—who intercon-nect (more or less effectively) as a group.

Building on the integral model, I call these four areas:

Intent	Content
Connect	Context

Of course we are living in all four quadrants at once. The lines and labels are artificial. However, they provide a wonderful map to understand the anatomy of meetings and to insure that, when we design or run them, we leave nothing out.

Take a breather, have a stretch. When you are back we'll look at each of those areas in more detail.

Intent

The Why of Meetings

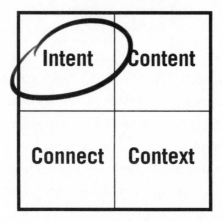

If you are in a meeting and wondering *what am I doing here?* it is time to pay attention to the top left quadrant.

Probably the most important moment in any meeting is one we don't notice. We walk straight past it in our hurry to get the job done. It comes just after the start. You've arrived (or phoned in), settled in your chairs and are just discussing what the meeting is about when ...

Stop.

Rewind.

There. Just before you say *what* the meeting is about. It's the *why* moment. It's the moment you can really energize the meeting, awaken, involve, and engage the participants. If you miss it, you are going to have to work that much harder for this meeting to succeed.

Even real engagement pros sometimes miss that moment. When the blockbuster film *The Gladiator* was first tested on audiences it had a so-so reaction. It was clearly a great action film, but the audiences felt something was missing. Then director Ridley Scott added a scene, right at the start. It goes something like this:

> *Fade up out of black.*
>
> *We hear an Asiatic woman's voice, keening. We are in close up on a man's hand drifting through a field of golden corn. We don't know it yet, but the hand belongs to the hero, the Roman general Maximus, played by Russell Crowe. We are soon to see him leading his loyal troops into battle against the marauding Germanic hordes. But here he is the farmer remembering the cornfields of his native land. We see a wedding ring on his finger. There is a distant peal of children's laughter and the thrum of a Spanish guitar.*

This scene is not telling us about *what* this person does, but *why* he does it; the inner motive and driving force beneath his actions. We are being introduced to this person from the left-hand side of the quadrant (his inner life) before we drop into his daily existence, actions, and plans.

In art it is absolutely common to make a distinction between a person's visible actions and their invisible emotional life. In business, less so.

The Gladiator is a soldier on the surface. But within he is a doting father and husband. Beneath the surface of the successful professional soldier is a professional farmer who cannot wait to fight one last battle and return to his beloved home and tend the crops.

Nietzsche claimed, "He who has a *why* can bear almost any *how*." The Gladiator certainly tests that—his To Do list is daunting. It includes beating the German army, galloping across Europe (too late) to save his family, surviving slavery, battling his way to eminence as a gladiator, making his way to Rome, and finally obtaining revenge by killing the evil Emperor. A full schedule indeed.

These *whats* all take energy. And where does the energy come from? His *why*. Though it is never said, we know from that first scene that the character is motivated not by belligerence, fury, bloodlust, or revenge—but love.

Meetings aren't movies. But the film-maker's basic principle of engaging your audience from the start is a great one for you to practice in your meetings.

By the way, if you look back at the opening of this book, you'll see me doing my best to grab your attention, just as you might at your next meeting. The first thing I did after saying hello was to mention the intent *to make the world a more interesting place*. Then I painted a picture, tried to excite you about the possibilities, gave you an idea of where we were going and why it was worth it.

These are all good techniques to steal and use at the start of every meeting. Start well, and you have a chance of finishing well.

What's the Intent of your meeting?

"Why are we meeting?" you ask, and people will usually tell you *what* the meeting is for; the objective. Knowing the objective is important but not sufficient. Not if you want to really meet. It is possible to have a perfectly plausible objective and still completely waste your time. Once you know the objective, you want to be asking yourself and others the real question: why is that objective important/useful/valuable/worth doing?

Or in other words, what is your intention?

You may have a meeting where the *objective* is to discuss sales figures. But discussion is not the ultimate intent. It's there *so that* you make great decisions, or navigate the next year well, or protect your investment, or ... or ... or ...

We are so used to collapsing intention and objective together we sometimes forget there's a difference. When you buy a lottery ticket, your *objective* is to win. Your *intention* is about what you will do with the winnings.

To discover, or uncover, the true intent of a meeting, I suggest clients use the question "so that ...?" to dig down into the objective to find the true intent buried beneath. It's what I like to call the "why of the why."

Let's work through a practical example.

Imagine a weekly team meeting. Let's say the objective is to *share information*. To help you identify the intent, I'd ask you to consider the value in doing that.

Me: You share information so that ...?

You: So that people all have the same information.

Me: OK. And what happens if they all have the same information?

You: We will all be on the same page?

Me: Hmmm. So that ...?

You: We can avoid errors, feel better connected, make better decisions ...?

Me: And if you did all those things what would that give you? So that ...?

And we keep descending the *so that* ... ladder until you hit what feels like the bottom, a *why* that sums up the heart of what you are doing and, most importantly, satisfies you.

You: To learn fast. Quicker than our competitors!

Me: Nice intent. Why not tell your colleagues that, next time you have your weekly meeting? Just before you get into the "stuff," remind people that this meeting is there to help you learn quicker and outthink your competition. I think you'll find that perks people up more than a plate of Chips Ahoy.

Here's another example, a real life one. I was working with a client, an auditor for a major bank, who described his monthly audit meeting as boring. His colleagues apparently felt the same way. We tried to excavate the deeper intent without much luck. He was getting stuck and I was getting frustrated. Then I remembered he had talked about his 18-year-old son and, on a hunch, I asked him if the boy drove a motorbike. Anton paled. He was clearly not happy. Why, Anton? "Because it's a danger-ous world out there," he replied with real passion. Anton was clearly very intent on being a good dad as well as a good auditor.

"So that ...?"

"So that I can keep things safe in a dangerous world!"

By a roundabout route we had uncovered the deeper intent of Anton's meeting and, possibly, his working life.

Which would you rather attend, a boring audit meeting or one that was going to help you *keep your company safe in a dangerous world*?

When you do this exercise you will find there are many ways down the ladder. And you can discover many different intents for the same meeting. In fact, I'd encourage you to refresh and renew the intent to keep the meeting alive. The important thing is to lift the manhole cover of the *objective* and start climbing down to find an *intent* you can tap into.

Intention Powers People as well as Meetings

"Knowing why" is also a key feature of successful teams and individuals.

Often a team meeting seems to lack power because the team itself is unclear about its reason for being. It doesn't know why it's there. If you think that's the problem, it can be very useful to ask the group the following question: *What is the work that only we can do?* Have a conversation about the unique contribution that *only* this precise collection of people can make to the business or organization. If you can't find one, it's maybe time to redesign the team, not the team meeting.

It's just as true for individuals. In this fast-moving, multi-matrixed, endlessly restructuring world of ours it's increasingly common for people to know the job they have but not the job they have to do. Roles are no longer as clear-cut as they were in the days of the baker, the blacksmith, and the cobbler. CEO, COO, CIO, director, manager, assistant—today's titles are so broad and generic you can find yourself unsure of what you are really doing and why. I do like the three questions Peter Drucker suggests you ask yourself:

> *What am I doing that does not need to be done at all?*
> *What am I doing that can done by someone else?*
> *What am I doing that only I can do?*

Once you have boiled your core activity down to its essence, I would ask a fourth question: "... and *why*?" When you are clear about the why of your actions, your actions will have real meaning and power. So will your meetings.

Powerful Intentions

The key to a powerful intention is to choose a powerful verb. "A new business meeting" is a noun, an object that just sits there on the page. When you describe it as "a meeting *to stimulate* new business" it comes alive. Verbs are all about action. The more dynamic the verb you choose, the more dynamic your meeting stands to be.

If you are stuck, here are some of the most common business intent verbs—plus a few nouns you can attach them to and, for the hell of it, some decorative adjectives.

VERBS	ADJECTIVES	NOUNS
BUILD	STRONG	CHANGES
CULTIVATE	IRRESISTIBLE	TEAMS
MANAGE	MARKET-BEATING	PRODUCTS
INVENT	INNOVATIVE	IDEAS

VERBS	ADJECTIVES	NOUNS
DEVELOP	IMPORTANT	INNOVATIONS
SOLVE	CRUCIAL	PEOPLE
PROTECT	WORLD-CHANGING	ROLES
GROW	PRACTICAL	PEOPLE
CLARIFY	ENDURING	VISIONS
GENERATE	SENSIBLE	PROFITS
DISCOVER	AUDACIOUS	LIVES
MAINTAIN	ATTRACTIVE	VALUE
MAXIMIZE	ESSENTIAL	UNDERSTANDING
LEARN	PASSIONATE	CUSTOMERS/CLIENTS
ENROLL	UNFORGETTABLE	CONNECTIONS
PROMOTE	SIGNIFICANT	PLANS
CREATE	WELCOME	JOY
INSURE	LASTING	ADVANTAGES
MAKE	HISTORIC	IMPACT

Intention helps you use your time better

If you can't find an intent, or it's not sufficiently important, kill the meeting. I mean it. Some meetings just go belly-up in this process. If you genuinely do the above exercise, and when you ask *so that what?* you draw a blank, the meeting is probably superfluous and/or could be done in another way. A great value of the intent-led approach is precisely that it exposes time-wasting meetings for culling.

Also, if you think about the meetings that take place in your life and organizations, you will see that many have similar intent and you can often usefully cluster these meetings together for better use of time.

Communicating the intent helps you and those attending understand why they are there—or, most importantly, why they may not need to be. A client was telling me that in her previous company the rule was that if you received an invitation to a meeting that did not contain an agenda you were obliged to refuse. Good idea, but I don't think an agenda is sufficient.

What I like to recommend is that when you receive a meeting invitation you send a courteous email asking the following two questions:

> *What is the intent of the meeting?*
> *And how can I specifically add value?*

If they don't reply, don't go. If they come back with an objective, not an intention, take them through the "so that ...?" process, or your version of it. And if you do both agree that the intention merits your attendance, do check the times you are required (between when and when), or you may be sitting through a whole meeting when only a part was relevant.

It's also a very useful guide to how long a meeting should be. Everyone complains that meetings go on too long. But that's because we often don't know why we are there in the first place. Let's face it:

> *If you don't know what you are doing, how will you know when you are done?*

In summary, if you are running the meeting you need to state the intent up front—as well as the objective. If you are attending someone else's meeting you need to ask them the intent. If they can't give one, don't go. If the meeting doesn't have a clear owner, or it's the kind of meeting "we have done for years," then work together to uncover its original intent or give it a new one.

Before we move into the world of Connect and actually meet some people, I want to leave you with a secret "Super Intent" I have discovered through my work in business around the world. It's an intent which works for every meeting you hold. It will serve your business and its people whatever sector you work in and whatever direction you want to go.

It is this. To create value.

The question I always ask clients—and have them ask themselves—is *how can this meeting create extraordinary value for everyone involved?* Not just value but *extraordinary* value. Not just for me, but for *everyone*, most particularly the other participants.

More about this one later. Suffice it to say if you really aim at creating value—be it monetary, cultural, personal, intellectual, social, commercial, communal, or spiritual—you are taking a short cut to designing Real Meetings. If it's *extraordinary* value, your colleagues will be lining up to get in. When people are lining up in the corridor for your meetings, camping overnight in sleeping bags waiting for the doors to open, we'll know we are creating extraordinary value. And it's the intention that gets us there.

Now let's meet some of those participants in person.

Connect

The Who of Meetings

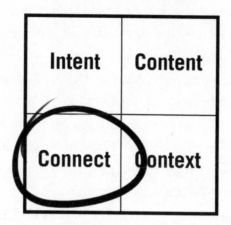

Getting the Casting Right

Like most fundamental principles, it's not complex. The key to the "who" of meetings is having the *right people* at your meetings for the *right reasons* and for the *right time*.

Like most simple things, however, it can be really hard to do. How often are the wrong people in the meeting? Or not enough of the right ones? How often is a meeting relevant to only a section of the attendees? And does all the above account for the fact that people are only minimally engaged, indeed barely conscious in meetings?

Three questions we will look at in this chapter are:

> *Who are these right people?*
> *How do you get them to your meeting?*

> *What do you do to keep them engaged, energized, and fully involved while they are there?*

The Right People for your Meeting

To use a film analogy, you want to get your "casting" right. You never saw a great movie with a lousy cast. And even a great star can kill a good movie if they are miscast.

Put Kevin Costner in a phantom baseball stadium (*Field of Dreams*)—great casting. Put him in tights (*Robin Hood, Prince of Thieves*) and you may be in trouble. Remember Mel Gibson as Hamlet, John Wayne as Genghis Khan, or kickass action heroine Angelina Jolie as long-suffering stay-at-home wife in *The Good Shepherd*? No? Precisely my point. Even geniuses make casting mistakes. Casting Marlon Brando as Vito Corleone in *The Godfather* was a masterstroke by director Francis Ford Coppola. Putting his daughter Sofia (a great director but a wooden actor) in *The Godfather Part III* nearly wrecked an otherwise fine film.

If you want to really meet—you need to get your cast right. And if you have done your work on the intent you will have a powerful guide to who these right people are.

... in the Right Roles

However skilled your casting, you can't make a great movie without the right roles to put your right people in.

What roles get played in meetings? It's a question I like to ask clients. And in their minds the cast list isn't very long. They'll identify the role of PRESENTER, essentially that's the person standing in front of the PowerPoint in the semi-darkness.

There's the AUDIENCE. This is an interesting term in its own right as it suggests a rather passive (literally "listening") role for most of the attendees.

There's often but not always a NOTE TAKER.

Finally, for the larger or more important meetings there's a CHAIRMAN/WOMAN, also known as CHAIRPERSON in gender-sensitive companies or simply THE CHAIR (though why anyone would want to be described as a piece of furniture is beyond me—however politically correct it may be).

And that's usually it. Unless you include today's important character parts:

THE TWITTERER—*their face says I am listening, their thumbs say I am texting.*

THE SIDE TALKER—*they comment about but don't actually contribute to your meeting.*

THE COVERT WORKER—*they are in the meeting but they are actually working on their laptop.*

THE SNOOZER—*they come in many varieties, including the skilled folks who can sleep deeply with eyes open—and mouth moving.*

THE SELF-PROMOTER—*like those annoying TV ads for low-cost credit or PVC window casings, they interrupt the flow of the meeting to plug themselves.*

I'd like to suggest a rather more helpful Dramatis Personae for you to choose from. This would include:

LEADER
Every meeting needs one (see below).

HOST
Not the same as Leader, as we shall see.

RECORDER
Someone to record what happens, so that those who don't attend but do have a stake in what is agreed can be kept up to date on progress. It's recorder rather than note taker because these days you can easily record what happens in audio and video files.

STAGE MANAGER/ORGANIZER
Dedicated to setting up the venue for success and keeping it effective while you are there.

PRESENTER(S)
These are the people who are making formal contributions to the meeting. Presenter is a good title as it reminds them and us to stay present. *Not drift off into needless detail or irrelevance ...*

PARTICIPANTS

That's everyone else in the meeting. If you are not, at some level, participating, you shouldn't be there. Meetings are not a spectator sport. *If they were, they'd need to be a whole lot more dynamic.*

You don't have to be making a lot of noise to be participating. Listening actively and asking just one great question can be as valuable as yards of blah-blah-blah.

FACILITATOR

A phrase I dislike, as it suggests someone who makes things easier. A good facilitator should also make things more difficult, particularly confronting people when they are settling for nearly *instead of* really *meeting.*

COACH

Successful teams always have coaches assessing the overall game and looking for improvements. Why not meetings too? I am often asked to sit on the sidelines in meetings, watching how things go, giving half-time feedback, and occasionally calling foul for low blows, clipping, and other meeting misdemeanors.

DEVIL'S ADVOCATE/IRRITANT

A good cast always has "bad" characters. Imagine Star Wars *with no Darth Vader, Bond with no Blofeld. A smart meeting caster will insure you have people in the room who are likely to challenge and provoke, not to disrupt the meeting but to "up the game." Seeing a group of like-minded colleagues sitting around agreeing is one of the most tiring sights in modern business. Make sure you include some grit to make the pearl.*

SPECIAL GUEST
A long-running TV series will often include special guests to keep the format fresh and stimulate the audience. You could think about including special guests in your cast list—people who would not normally sit around your table but who have fresh ideas to offer (see below).

You may look at the list above and think that's a lot of people. I should stress that you don't need all these roles at every meeting and that some can be amalgamated (e.g. recorder/organizer/timekeeper). Whatever your final cast list, it is important that you think about how diverse individuals can make specific contributions within a connected whole.

By the way, you will find that when participants have a role they tend to be more engaged. That's true even if the role is quite mundane. I was in a meeting session the other day and saw that one of the participants was about to drift off. Her head was nodding and then jerking back with a face that said, "I wasn't dozing, I wasn't!" So I asked her to be timekeeper. That meant, every 20 minutes, she had to "ting" a hotel reception bell that I carry with me. I like to do this to remind meeting participants it's time to hit their own internal "refresh button." When the least "present" participant became the person in charge of maintaining Presence, she had a stake in what was happening and woke up fast.

Who is Leading the Meeting?

If a meeting is in trouble, one of the first questions to ask is "Who is leading this meeting?" If there's no clear answer, or you only get blank stares, you know you have hit gold.

Meetings need to be led. All meetings. A meeting without leadership is like a high-performance 4x4 without a steering wheel. You are going off-road all right, but not in the unbounded adventure sense; more in the "get wrapped around a tree" sense. To put it another way, there has to be at least one person in the room (or on the phone) who knows why you are all there and is prepared to guide you through the time you have together.

I would argue that if you look around a meeting and can't see a leader, you should put your hand up and make sure that person is YOU.

The leaderless meeting is becoming more common as many companies seek to move away from an over-hierarchical past toward a culture that is more collaborative, consensual, and horizontal. "Let's dispense with the formality," goes the thinking. "We don't need anyone to lead this meeting. The team can lead itself. We will just get together and work it out ..." This is compounded by *politeness*. It is seen as just bad manners to impose leadership in a horizontal situation where everyone's opinion is as valid as everyone else's.

Another reason meetings are *leaderless* is that they are *ownerless* too. When you ask, "Whose meeting is this?" people shrug or point at everyone else. Very often people don't know or can't remember why the meeting is being held, and no one wants to take responsibility. I call these "orphan meetings." And in this age of Outlook and other calendar software they are becoming more and more prevalent. Someone, somewhere sends a meeting invitation to an unfiltered list and, at the flick of button, another orphan meeting is born into an uncaring world.

I do encourage "support" staff to be vigilant when they are asked to send or accept an invitation to what looks or feels like an "orphan" meeting.

When people refer to the "leader," they usually mean the person who tells us what comes next and how long we have left. That is helpful, but it's not leadership. To explain meeting leadership better, I want to draw a distinction between *hosting* a meeting and *running* one.

Hosting v Running

These are two distinct aspects of leading a meeting—*running* it and *hosting* it—which we tend to collapse together. And this is causing problems.

Imagine you have invited some friends over for dinner. Nothing fancy. A few drinks, some Jamie Oliver idiot-proof starters, a barbeque, and one of those pre-bought desserts. You're well prepared, with the ingredients lined up, wine and beer in the fridge, charcoal at a perfect temperature, when the doorbell goes. You welcome the first guests, give them a drink and then pop on the kebabs. The bell goes again. You welcome the next guests, give them a drink and introduce them to the first arrivals, have a laugh, put some music on—and notice the smell of burning meat. No worries. Just douse the flames, toss the first kebabs and prepare the second round. Then the phone goes. It's a couple who are running late. You balance your cell on your shoulder as you put the second round of kebabs on. Then the bell rings again ...

We've all done this, or something like it. We are trying to socialize with our eye on the cooking and to cook while trying to carry on a conversation with friends through the smoke. We are *hosting* and *running* the evening at the same time. The result is, we don't do either well.

"There speaks a man!" I can imagine the woman reader thinking to herself. Yes, it is a truism that women are better at multitasking in this way than men, but however your chromosomes are arranged, the situation is still a stretch.

A very similar thing is happening when the person leading the meeting tries to host and run the meeting at the same time. Remember our four quadrants? If we split ourselves into two parts, one *hosting* and the other *running* the meeting, you'll see they view the meeting map from quite different angles.

If you are being the Host, you are thinking ...

INTENT	CONTENT
Set a powerful intent powerfully	What isn't being said that should be?
CONNECT	CONTEXT
Check how the participants are connecting (including on the phone) What's the mood of the group today?	Keep the business context in participants' minds

WILL THERE BE DONUTS?

If you are running things, you are thinking ...

INTENT	CONTENT
Has the intent been set?	What needs to be covered today? And what can be taken offline for the next meeting?
CONNECT	CONTEXT
Are all the participants present? And if not, how do I get hold of them to check when they are joining?	Is the air-conditioning too cold, why is the line crackling and when are the donuts coming?

Wherever possible, I suggest you split these two important roles between two (or more) people.

The person who "owns" the meeting should host it. They set the intention and are accountable for the design and outcome. Often this will be the most senior executive, but this shouldn't be a default decision. Where a meeting is owned by a more junior person, they should absolutely host the meeting. And the more senior figure should be treated as an active participant.

To insure the host is free to concentrate on their central role, all the tasks of running of the meeting should be handled by someone else. That includes finding, booking, and preparing a room; keeping time; noting important points; navigating through the agenda; even communicating logistical information about bathrooms and fire alarms.

To really lead a meeting, think about distributing the various roles of leadership between different people in this way. At the very least, consider having the most senior person NOT physically running the meeting, but instead playing the vital role of Host.

Rotating Presidency

In a repeated meeting where the host remains the same, I'd encourage you to rotate the running of the meeting between different participants. It can be quite energizing if no one knows who is going to run the meeting until they are chosen at the start. This encourages all participants in a meeting to turn up prepared to be active in a "hands-ready" state of mind.

It's a phrase I remember from the early years of parenting when we watched our toddlers "furniture-surfing" their way around the house. You can choose to be a *hands-off* parent, allowing your child to fall and pick themselves up. Or a *hands-on* one, who is so smotheringly attentive the toddlers barely toddle. *Hands-ready* means you give the wayward child the freedom to get into difficulty but you are there to support them if and when they do. I've found this middle way works well, as a principle not just for parenting, but also for team accountability. Ultimately, every member of the team is there to "catch the baby if it falls."

Mates or Allies? Grit in the Oyster

I heard a story about explorer Robert Swan who, after failing in a solo attempt at the South Pole, brought together an elite squad of people to support his next expedition. The team he assembled included the best cook, medic, dog handler, and navigator he could find. Not long into the trek, he found himself stomping around in the snow, fuming. Swan's fellow adventurers were driving him mad. Skilled they were, but not his kind of people. One was permanently grumpy, another snored, another had an odd sense of humor, while a third had no sense of humor at all. They had different perspectives and attitudes from his own. As he stomped around in the snow he wondered why he had not brought his friends. And then it hit him. "I could have brought my friends with me. But I would have died."

Mates tell you what you want to hear. Allies tell you what you need to hear.

It's an instructive story if you are wondering whom to pull together for a meeting, particularly when the stakes are high and there is a real problem to crack. The tendency might be to bring together your "nearest and dearest," trusted colleagues who get on and work well together. Great, but caution! The people you are leaving out of your list, the awkward ones who don't agree with you, the dissenting voices, may be just the people to insure you "don't die." They may be precisely ones who force you to think about things differently, see the angle that has been eluding you. We all have our blind spots—teams as well as individuals—and it takes others, including those we may not like a lot, to illuminate them.

When I asked Barbara Stocking to describe one of her best-ever meetings, she picked one where the casting was perfect.

One of my most satisfying meetings ever was in Jakarta airport in the aftermath of the Tsunami. It was all about the changeover from emergency to a more ongoing development. We had pretty well every level of management there—we had the guy running the program, the guy taking it over, the regional director, my No. 2 and the chairperson. That was absolutely fantastic because within just two hours we were able to look at all the past problems and where the program was going.

We didn't have every relevant person, but a small group that represented all the relevant levels, from people who really knew the situation on the ground to the top leadership. So we knew we weren't making decisions that didn't make sense in the field. And they knew they had the top support and this was a once-and-for-all meeting.

If the key people aren't in the room it can be a disaster. In Oxfam, because everyone is traveling all the time, you often have meetings with one or two key people not there. And someone standing in for them who either can't negotiate the decision or can't be held to the decision once it's made. I often say to my staff, "If people are going to stand in for you, they have to have the proper negotiating brief so they can really say yes and hold the organization to that commitment."

The meeting wasn't without its "grit." We had these two big chaps—I mean physically large as well as important— between whom there had been a certain amount of, shall we say, dynamic. But just by practically working through what was going to happen we made enormous progress in just a couple of hours.

Everyone was very open. No hiding about anything. Everyone put their backs into it. It was great.

Special Guest: the Art of the Unexpected Invitee

Special guests, unexpected arrivals, mystery contributors—they all serve to add depth and richness to a meeting.

Here are six examples I have seen where surprise casting totally revolutionized a meeting.

1. Hack attack

Ericsson was keen to launch a range of fancy new internet-based technologies at the youth consumer market. Though this was not a focus group or market research event, we couldn't resist inviting a club of 12-year-old hackers to join the meeting we designed for them. One potential product after another bit the dust as the hackers—this global company's future market—showed how the application was redundant, irrelevant to them, or just too expensive. I will always remember the expression on the face of one enthusiastic engineer as he asked the kids how much they would be willing to pay for a product they did seem interested in. "Pay?" responded one hacker. "I wouldn't pay anything for it. I thought it was free!" It was an uncomfortable meeting, but it must have saved the company considerable sums they would otherwise have spent on developing valid but ultimately unsaleable products.

2. The Cardboard Kid

I have noticed that children rarely attend business meetings. I can only assume they have much more important things to do on Facebook. It's a shame, though, particularly when the business is talking about youth or making decisions that will affect them in the future. I often suggest to clients that they leave a chair free at the meeting and imagine a 12-year-old is sitting there. A cardboard cut-out helps. You'd be amazed at how the acronyms disappear and the language gets clearer as board members seek to make themselves understood by their under-age non-Exec.

3. Mothers' Day

Menopause plays hell with your skin, I am told. Procter & Gamble saw an opportunity for a new face cream and asked us via their advertising company to organize a workshop to explore the creative possibilities. I agreed, on one (slightly fresh) condition: everyone had to bring their mom to the meeting. It seemed a good idea. Who better than moms to advise on a product aimed at them? To my surprise, the client agreed. So did the moms, mine included. It was a meeting like no other I can remember. I swear there was a moment when my mother suggested I "sit down" while she and the other moms quietly took over. It was an unforgettable (!) and very useful meeting. One insight—the moms revealed: *they don't try to look good for men but for other women*—changed the whole tack of the promotional campaign to support this product. By fully including these valuable people in the meeting—rather than speculating about them—the client created real value for everyone involved.

4. The Satisfied Customer

If you are looking for a job with lots of stroke risks, I wouldn't recommend the front line of the U.K. employment service. It's incredibly hard work dealing with jobseekers in various forms of stress and distress. The pay is not great and the hours are demanding, while the pressure is unremitting and the plaudits are few and far between. Yet the year's project we ran with them was one of the most touching of my career so far. And here's why.

These civil servants worked hard without any real appreciation or recognition for what they were doing. They arrived tired, jaded, and skeptical about "innovation."

So, at each meeting we held, we would always invite at least one "mystery guest," someone who had been helped by JobCentre Plus, against the odds, to find and keep gainful employment. This included the rough sleeper who was now a coffee entrepreneur, the laid-off carpenter now running a bustling Jamaican catering company, and, perhaps most poignant of all, the young single mother who, thanks to a part-time job, was able to take the first family vacation of her young children's lives. There was not a dry eye in the house. And the emotions (pride, pleasure, joy, satisfaction) charged up those meetings, so we all had the energy to begin innovating.

5. Unsung Heroes, Missing Voices?

We'll talk more about this later, but do be sure to include "support staff." The PAs, back office staff and functions (how I dislike that impersonal term) that provide the backbone of the organization often don't get invited to meetings where they can make a really valuable contribution. I tend to think it's because, when they do their job well, they actually become rather invisible.

A lawyer friend offered me a great example of the huge effect support staff can have on the bottom line. His law firm had a receptionist with an almost magical gift for recognizing the voices of their clients. She'd only need to hear someone's voice once to be able to recall them by name many months later. You can imagine the effect it had on a client or potential client to be greeted warmly and personally on the second call. The lawyers appreciated this skill, certainly, but weren't too upset when the receptionist mentioned she was moving on to a new job. They were a lot more alarmed when over the following year their client acquisition and retention took a severe knock.

As my colleague, the executive mentor Tom Cummings, wisely says, *ventures founder when one party overvalues their own contribution and undervalues the contribution of others.* "Support staff" (even the title boxes them in) see the world and your business's place in it through very different eyes. If you are wise you will capitalize on, rather than marginalize, the perspective offered by the unseen and often unsung heroes that actually run your organizations.

6. The Spouse Grouse

None of us likes the idea of segregation. Which is why I am often baffled at larger meetings and conferences when the employees are directed to the business session and the spouses and "significant others" are directed to—go shopping. Now it is very likely the spouses are pleased to be avoiding that two-hour PowerPoint on tax planning, but that is not the point. I think there is a strong case for involving non-work relationships in many business-only meetings.

The first time I was asked to organize an offsite meeting, I included spouses—because I didn't know you weren't supposed to. It culminated with a do-it-yourself entertainment, where the participants were cast and crew. I remember vividly a rather slight woman scampering 20 feet up into the rigging to man the spotlight. "For once in my life," she declared, "I am going to be the one who decides whether my husband gets the limelight or not."

The Art of Invitation: or How do you get the right people to the meeting?

OK, let's assume you have identified the right people for your meeting. Now you have to get them to attend. To be a successful casting director, after all, it's not enough that you can spot the right people. You have to persuade them to say yes.

And that wooing process begins with the invitation. I'd suggest a really successful meeting experience begins the moment you send the invitation, when you plant the seed in the audience's mind. You are creating meaning. You are building anticipation. If you wait for your meeting to start when your meeting actually starts, you may be too late to create the engagement you need.

Most people think the function of the invitation is just to inform attendees about the meeting.

THE ANATOMY OF MEETINGS

DEAR TEAM MEMBER
REMINDER
Subject: Team Meeting. 0900–1200
Room H4963
See agenda attached
Best regards
PA to David

In these days of info glut and time pressure, attention is a scarce resource. You need to *market* or *enroll* or *seduce* potential attendees if you want them to show up.

DEAR NICOLE,
I wanted you to know we are holding a team meeting next Thursday to finalize and sign off the new offer. We are doing this now so everything is underway before the holidays. The intention is that the competition will be playing catch-up for the rest of the year.

    The work you are doing on customer attitudes is vital to the decision. Could you spend 45 minutes sharing your insight on this 10.00 to 10.45? You are welcome to attend the rest of the meeting but the choice is yours.

    If you really don't have time we can do this without you—but it would be way less effective and enjoyable.
From David

I know which invitation I would say yes to. In the second you have stated intent, set context, established why their attendance is valuable and for what part of the meeting.

The right people for the right time

When was the last time you went to the theater or the movies and everyone was in every scene? Imagine. Hamlet walks on at the start followed by a ghost, his whole family, Ophelia, and the entire Danish army. The writer and director and actors understand that it would be bad storytelling, not to mention a very poor use of resources, to use the whole cast throughout. Impact in a drama is not (necessarily) measured in airtime. Actors know they can leave an enormous impression when their presence is used sparingly and at just the right moment. Indeed economy often heightens effect. I saw a performance of *The Ice Man Cometh* in which Kevin Spacey was starring—but playing a character who does not appear on stage for 50 minutes. When he finally arrived, the impact was immense. People in show business have no problem with appearing at the end of Act Two, as they know that in a well-constructed piece their part is making a specific and unique contribution to the whole. Conversely, if they are on stage too much they can "disappear."

Makes sense? So why do we do exactly the opposite in meetings? A cast of characters assemble (often not sure why they are there) and sit through the whole thing. By definition large chunks of the meeting are irrelevant, and no wonder people start sneaking a look at their emails. Far better if you invite people to take a specific part in a meeting, for a specific part of that meeting.

I'm told the academic world has a real penchant for over-casting their meetings. A friend of mine who is a Professor of Fine Art at one of the world's leading art colleges has told me of the time recently when he found himself sitting on a committee of 15 people to decide which tutors would receive a small bursary, a few thousand pounds—to invest in their own personal development. "I couldn't help pointing out to them that our combined time was costing way more than the entire fund we had available for the bursaries, and suggested instead that we delegate responsibility to three staff, representing academic, technical, and administration, and review the matter after 12 months. How much of a mistake could they make? If these folk mess up, we can always replace them. I think people can become fearful of delegating and so overcompensate by, as in this case, over-staffing committees."

Not inviting the wrong people is as important as inviting the right ones ...

I really do think one of the reasons the wrong people end up at meetings is politeness. That's the word we Anglo-Saxons use to mean a fear of confrontation and/or appearing to spare the feelings of others while in fact protecting ourselves from the discomfort of telling the truth.

Forgive me, but I think there is a serious case of "I won't mention it if you don't mention it" going on here. Many is the time that client A has told me they have to invite client B, or B will feel left out, snubbed, or offended. And then I will bump into B, who tells me they'd rather not attend but don't feel they can refuse because this will offend, upset, or undermine A. It's one of those times when candidness—a real conversation—would be more effective than politeness.

If it is not misplaced manners, then it's politics and careerism. People show up at meetings because they feel power or kudos is involved.

And the wrong person may be YOU

Time for a tiny peek in the mirror. How many meetings do you say yes to because it makes you feel just a little bit important? Especially if there are other "important" people there. I ask because, as much as people complain about meetings, I do often detect just a hint of self-aggrandizement and smugness in the complaint.

"God, I am exhausted. It's been meetings, meetings, meetings. Those annoying people from the World Bank. Then the UN, and finally that Clooney guy—he really does go on."

If you think there's any chance you might be saying yes to irrelevant meetings—or even gatecrashing ones you are not invited to—because they are a notch on your personal power totem, I strongly suggest you make yourself a card like the one below and recite the mantra that goes with it:

I am already an Important Person
Attending more meetings does not make me more important
I say NO to unnecessary meetings

Context

The Where and When of Meetings

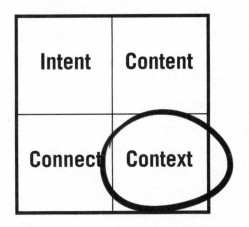

Context creates meaning and meaning creates ...

Imagine for a moment it is your lunch hour and you have joined a long line at the bank because you need to deposit a check. The only teller is a junior undergoing training and nothing seems to be happening. Time is short, but now is the only time you have. So you tut inwardly and wait your turn. Suddenly a man bumps into your shoulder and walks straight past you to the front of the line. How do you feel? The man withdraws some cash, turns around and you see he is wearing dark glasses and carrying a white stick. Now how do you feel? You decided to give up on the teller and leave the bank when you suddenly see the blind man take off his sunglasses and vault lightly into an open-topped Porsche which he drives away from the disabled bay with a roar. Now how do you feel?

This story beautifully illustrates the fact that *context creates meaning*. At each point the context changed, and this changed how you understood the experience you were having. Your emotional responses—from annoyance, to guilt, to rage—were also conditioned by the context. It is the frame we put around reality that lets us know what is going on. As Aldous Huxley put it, "Experience isn't what happens to you, it is what you do with what happens to you."

We are lost in a vacuum. Context gives us meaning. And what does meaning give, especially to a meeting? Energy. You only need to have sat in one meaningless meeting to know how sapping that feels. Meetings are experiences framed by context. Frame them well and your meetings will be meaningful and energized.

There are two main types of context I want us to look at. There's the Big Picture and the Physical Setting.

How Big is Your Big Picture?

> *I am happy to join with you today in what will go down in history as the greatest demonstration for freedom in the history of our nation.*

Not a bad piece of context-setting from Martin Luther King, Jr. on August 28 1963. And on he goes:

> *Five score years ago, a great American, in whose symbolic shadow we stand today, signed the Emancipation Proclamation. This momentous decree came as a great*

beacon light of hope to millions of Negro slaves who had been seared in the flames of withering injustice. It came as a joyous daybreak to end the long night of their captivity.

You can hear a pin drop.

But one hundred years later, the Negro still is not free. One hundred years later, the life of the Negro is still sadly crippled by the manacles of segregation and the chains of discrimination. One hundred years later, the Negro lives on a lonely island of poverty in the midst of a vast ocean of material prosperity. One hundred years later, the Negro is still languishing in the corners of American society and finds himself an exile in his own land. So we have come here today to dramatize a shameful condition. In a sense we have come to our nation's capital to cash a check.

Not only fabulous context-setting but also a powerful intent to boot (*we are here to cash a check*). Before getting into detail, Martin Luther King creates a huge canvas for an epic gathering (*the greatest demonstration of freedom in history*). He gives the big picture first.

It's a very powerful technique, whether you are addressing a million demonstrators in Washington or a small staff meeting in Cleveland. It gives the meeting energy, a sense of purpose. Without it the meeting can easily collapse inwards—as so many do—and wind up focusing on the internal minutiae and not the external world where real life happens and real customers live.

Keeping the wider business context in mind also helps you calibrate the level of urgency that should attach to the meeting. These days everything is urgent. And it's all simultaneously clamoring for your undivided attention. But is it important? Keeping the context in mind helps you dial up or down to the appropriate level of attention the topic deserves.

If a vegetable seller wants to show off a red apple, she may place it on a mat of green fake grass. You don't notice the green background. All you see is the vivid red of the apple. Meetings are like that. They gain definition when set against the background of the business.

So when you are planning or attending the meeting, it is important to keep what is happening in the business, the market, and the wider world in your peripheral vision, as it were. Even a humdrum meeting gains substance and meaning if people can connect the effort they are making to the larger story.

I do think this is a principal and growing function of leaders: to place ordinary events and everyday actions in the greater story, so we understand the part we are playing in the whole.

Oxfam's Barbara Stocking is constantly being dropped into meetings around the globe, often in very pressured situations. How does she get "on terms" with the people she is meeting? "First of all is always context. What is the history, how did we get here? It's how you establish a human relationship before you start negotiating on anything. That's got to be the way."

Big Picture Shrinking?

One of the reasons we don't talk much about what's happening outside our business is that we don't spend enough time looking outside to find out. Even in these info-glutted times, it's easy to concentrate so much on your area of business that you lose contact with what's going on outside your "patch."

I remember the CFO of an international catering organization asking me how to have more engaging meetings. He was good at leaping to the detail, but was missing the connection with the bigger picture. I noticed he had a stack of magazines by his desk. But they were all about his industry.

He's in and out of airports and railroad stations all the time (his company specializes in transportation catering), so I suggested that every time he passes a newsstand, he should buy himself a magazine he would never normally read. He may not be interested in *Sailing Weekly* or the *Recycling Times* or *Twelve New Ways to Make Ratatouille*—but his customers may very well be.

Because he started reading, noting, and clipping, he now has a much broader perspective and can start his meetings being more informed (... *I don't know if you know the statistics on package recycling* ...), more connected to what's going on (... *there's an innovation in adventure vacations that I think we can all learn from* ...) and more interesting (... *I was chopping tomatoes the other day and I thought our business is a bit like ratatouille* ...).

You can try this technique yourself if you feel your own big picture has shrunk. Ask people in your company to recommend what they are reading and/or what they feel you should be reading. Listen to new radio stations (internet radio stations make this simple). When you are choosing which TV shows to watch, choose a few which someone completely different from you would watch. When you are out and about in your business, listen to people's stories, not just the facts. Get the outsiders' perspective and draw on this when you are seeking to engage people within your business.

When you bring the outside world into your meetings in this way, you create context, meaning, and energy. You are reminding everyone that, in however small a way, what happens here affects what happens out there. You are not in a vacuum, pushing paper around and munching cookies laced with trans-fats. You are doing something that matters. There is something at stake.

If you want to go one stage further and really up the ante, you can try a technique I often use with team meetings. I call it ...

The World is Watching

Before you start a meeting, hand out some blank sheets of paper or index cards to all the participants. Ask them to consider: "Who, aside from us participants, has a stake in the outcome of this meeting?" Encourage them to think widely, beyond the obvious business boundaries. The lists of meeting "stakeholders" will often include:

> *absent team members*
> *reports*
> *the Board*
> *partner companies*
> *shareholders*

> *the workforce*
> *customers*
> *customers' customers*
> *our future customers*
> *loved ones (where the meeting has a significant bearing on future planning)*

This is already useful in giving even humdrum meetings an extra significance. But to really land the point, I ask people to draw a face or name of each of these characters on a piece of paper or card. We prop or stick these "puppets" up all over the room, creating a virtual audience for the meeting itself. It sounds weird, I know, but under the gaze of these symbolic faces it feels as if the world really is watching. I have seen meetings gain significant pace, urgency, and relevance—all thanks to a couple of hundred oddly scribbled characters "watching from the sidelines."

Bringing the Outside In

Oddly, there is a reverse phenomenon which I call a Home Alone meeting, where it seems that everything important is happening somewhere "out there." As a result the meeting is stymied. There are several unspoken attitudes that can help create this effect:

> *We'd like to agree this but the CEO is not available*
> *We think this is a good idea, but of course Head Office won't let us*
> *We can't really proceed until X (the senior leader) gets back from Guadeloupe*

❯ *The guys at IT are really to blame, but they never pick up the phone ...*

All this may be true. But—and it's a big but—the Home Alone meeting has a disempowered atmosphere that can drain energy and evaporate morale. If ever you feel you are in one of these, you may find it useful to write up the following words in big, fluorescent letters—possibly across your forehead: THERE IS NO "OUT THERE" OUT THERE.

You are asking your colleagues to imagine, for a moment, that you are the only people in the business. That all the problems are in the room, along with all the solutions. I have seen teams burst into life doing this exercise. It puts the power slap-bang in the middle of the meeting, stops all that draining finger-pointing which saps initiative and makes everyone feel like victims.

Context Clash

There are times when the outside context just forces its way into the room whether you like it or not. It can be profoundly dramatic. I'll never forget a meeting about Risk and Change at Zurich Insurance's headquarters being interrupted by a director arriving late with the shocking news that a plane had hit the World Trade Center.

At the other end of the spectrum, sometimes you can't help but laugh. The motivational speaker Steve McDermott tells a wonderful story of a software company's business meeting at which he was booked to speak.

The theme of the event was something like Together We Can, and they had booked me to really rev the employees up. When I arrived, I noticed the management in a huddle, looking worried. Then the CEO walks on stage to tell the crowd that their company has gone into receivership. Not only had they gone bust, he explained, but "all your company cars are going to be repossessed by the leasing company, so please hand in your keys at the end of the day." There wasn't a sound. Everyone was looking at him with their mouths open. Silence. And a banner saying "Together We Can." With that he turned to me and announced, "Now please welcome our motivational speaker for this afternoon—Steve McDermott!"

That's what you call a perfect set-up—in the least helpful sense of the word!

Context and Time

The other aspect of the Bigger Picture we need to be aware of is Time. Meetings are often talked about as events. I prefer to think of a meeting as an experience that starts before the actual meeting begins and continues after it's done. Not a point, or a wave, but a point *on* a wave.

Real meetings begin long before anyone turns up or logs in. I have been involved with some meetings where you start planting the seeds months in advance. Like a good cook, you are making sure that by the time your diners arrive, everything is almost ready.

Reading in Advance

Pre-reading—or (p)research, as Rachel, one of our producers, likes to describe it—is key to meeting success. The most complained-about aspect of poor meeting discipline is "turning up unprepared." As Ron the Consultant puts it:

> *Meeting materials have to be distributed in advance. And read. That way you can start the meeting with "Any questions about the material?" If people actually did this, it would slice most information meetings down to 10 minutes.*

One tip: between sending out the invitations and the meeting itself, ask the attendees (by mail, phone, or in person) to answer a question or two that will help them start thinking in the right direction and give you valuable insight about what is on their minds.

For example: "Thanks for accepting the invitation. What, specifically, is it about the invitation that encouraged you to accept?" Or: "If we could do just one thing in the meeting, what would you want that to be?" Questions like these help you understand whether what you are offering is what your colleagues are looking for. If it's not, then refine. It's primitive market research.

Meeting success takes adequate preparation; in some cases, literally years. Jim Garrison, who set up the Gorbachev Foundation/U.S.A. (now the State of the World Forum), was telling me about the *five years* of preparation that preceded his first epic meeting with the Big Man.

Often a meeting needs to be viewed as part of an overarching strategy towards a particular goal. In the Perestroika era I spent five years working in Moscow, developing relationships with the Central Committee, with the Politburo, with high-level soviets but I had a single intent that I wanted to meet Mikhail Gorbachev, who I felt at that time was one of the great historical figures of the 20th century. When I finally ended up meeting him, I was ready. I entered the meeting with all the intent and energy that had incubated for all that time. I came in and we clicked. It was December 17th, 1991. I was the last foreigner to meet with Gorbachev in his Kremlin office. Then we had a meeting in January 1992 after he had resigned his presidency. I would say those two meetings were crucial in actually determining the next ten years of my life.

Out of those meetings, he agreed with my vision and asked me to set up the Gorbachev Foundation in the United States. And that led to all kinds of projects, meetings with wonderful and diverse people, and ultimately a State of the World Forum, which lasts to the present day.

That's an example of literally choreographing strategy in order to get to a meeting, and then fill the meeting with such content that it really shapes the future.

We'll come to content, but for now I want to look at the third type of context we need to be aware of—the Physical Context of meetings.

The Physical Context: Setting Shapes Outcomes

All meetings happen in a space (virtual spaces in the case of virtual meetings), and this physical setting shapes the experience and the outcome more than many of us realize.

Imagine you are called to address an important meeting. You enter the room to find your colleagues filling two rows of chairs in straight lines facing you. Now imagine entering the same room to discover the same people and chairs arranged in a circle with one space left for you. Notice the difference in how these two options would make you feel. One setting evokes a theater and makes you feel like you need to give a performance. The other setting evokes a campfire get-together and makes you feel like you want to have a conversation.

The people who run commercial meeting venues have cottoned on to this and now offer formats like "theater-style" and "café-style" seating. One tends to make us more attentive to the presentation. The other can promote interaction. The converse is also true. Trying to promote interaction in a theater-style set-up goes against the archetypal grain, so don't be surprised if you find people unusually hesitant to interact when they are sitting in neat rows. And if you have ever tried to address a room full of people at round tables as though they were a unified audience, you will have noticed how difficult it can be. Not only are you talking to the back of people's heads (those who are not twisting round to see you), but the room seems to be more gaps than people. In the theater we talk about elan-holes—places in the audience where the energy seems to disappear into a vacuum. Performers will tell of the importance of connecting with the audience and how a good connection seems to draw a good performance out of them. It is not a one-way transaction: the energy feels like it is flowing between stage and audience in a genuinely shared experience.

As a designer and engineer of real meetings you should remember that we humans are creatures who sense space and are deeply influenced by the environment around us. Change the setting, and not just the meeting but the whole meeting culture can change, too.

Sawing up the Boardroom Table

When I first met the CEO of insurers Skandia International, Andre Oszmann, his company was a part of Skandia Group, itself owned by the South African giant Old Mutual. Andre had a big vision for SI, wanting it to become a division in its own right with its own distinctive culture, financial autonomy, and modus operandi. SI manages the money of high net worth individuals around the world, so it needs to be a lot more engaging, innovative, and personal than is the norm in the insurance sector.

It's a people business. Not that you'd have known that at first glance if you'd been standing in their rather soulless, corporate offices back in 2006. There was a buzz, certainly. Andre had gathered a pretty go-getting group around him. But their energy was dissipated by the conventional setting and traditional office routines.

Andre and his team wanted things to change and accepted that central to a new way of working was a new way of meeting.

Andre is what you might call an "early adopter," someone who tends to say yes when they encounter something new that appeals to them. So when I suggested they saw up the boardroom table, he took me seriously, and the mahogany monster dominating the boardroom was summarily dismantled.

A symbolic act, perhaps, but one which communicated a very real change. Andre and his team didn't just flirt with new meeting ideas, they really practiced. For example, every meeting began with a statement of intent. If it wasn't clear or engaging enough, the meeting was scrapped. To manage energy in longer meetings, the cookies and Cokes disappeared and were replaced by protein bars and water.

Before conference calls were held, the participants would spend a couple of minutes silently gathering their thoughts and/ or "tuning in" to the colleagues or customers around the world they were just about to speak to.

"Our meetings became much more focused, outcome-orientated and productive," says Andre. "Everyone was fully engaged and forgot about their BlackBerry; they were having fun driving the business together and it changed the game."

Word spread fast, and when the head of OM flew in on a rare fact-finding mission he deliberately re-routed his flight so he could meet SI "in their natural habitat." Within six months, Skandia International were a business in their own right, with distinctive profile in the OM Group that remained commercially strong even through the toughest times of the credit crunch.

I wouldn't claim the new approach to meetings was the cause of this success, but according to Andre, SI's transformation wouldn't have been possible without sawing up that table.

Meetings v Architects

The US architect Philip Johnson was a visionary, no doubt. But he has a lot to answer for. If he hadn't visited Europe in the 1930s, got all excited by the stripped-down, Bauhaus approach and come back to America thinking that is how buildings ought to look (as well as being efficient, quick, and cheap to build), we might now be working and meeting in spaces designed for the spatially aware animals that we are. We did not evolve to spend hours in artificial light, sitting slumped around a table munching refined sugar, and trying to do our best work as the air-conditioning sucks the life out of us.

Developers have started to call their anonymous office boxes evocative things like Savana, Apollo, Picasso, and Summer, presumably in the hope of imbuing them with some character, but the truth is that the standard working environment in which most business is done owes more to the cost advantages of modular building methods than any esthetic logic.

I do think it's fascinating to consider why the modern office looks the way it does. For example, the office desk. Why is it rectilinear, not circular, kidney- or inkblot-shaped? In the first decade of the twentieth century the U.S. was gripped by an enthusiasm for time-and-motion studies and the scientific management views of F. W. Taylor. The idea emerged that managers needed to start actively directing employees' work. (Whether you think this was an advance or a setback depends largely on whether or not you are a manager!)

This active supervision was hard to accomplish from behind a massive Victorian roll-top desk. Enter the "Modern Efficiency

Desk," introduced by The Equitable Life Insurance Company in 1915. It had a flat top and drawers below, so nothing would obstruct the manager's beady gaze.

And where do cubicles come from? It turns out the answer isn't sheep-pens, warehouses, or battery farming. By the 1960s the U.S. had discovered that open plan had its problems. The main difficulty appeared to be that if you can see everything your people are doing, they can see everything you are doing, too. To bring some discretion and privacy back into the workplace, in 1964 the Herman Miller company created the Action Office, which later evolved into the cubicle office that has spread across the globe like Japanese knotweed.

And hotels! Hotel designers the world over clearly take the least attractive space available, the bit they don't know what else to do with, the place that residents would never stay and isn't good for the parking lot, and rename it the Conference Facility. Its features include endless low-ceilinged, airless, windowless rooms with poor air-conditioning and worse sound insulation. Businesses then pay fabulous sums of money to rent these spaces and attempt to do high-quality work in them. I feel like shouting, "You are holding the most important meeting of the year in a furniture storage room!"

I shouldn't complain. No, really, I shouldn't.

Last year I was holding a workshop in North Carolina, helping a multinational client that wanted to cure itself of "meeting-itis." I was lambasting the venue, pointing out the perversity of creating dual PowerPoint screens that looked like two huge blank eyes, and the low ceilings, and the clumsy, connection-obstructing tables that were wired in and bolted to the floor. I was on a roll, being egged on by the audience to really let rip. "What the hell were they thinking when they designed this?" While I was in mid-diatribe a man raised his hand at the back. "Do you have a question?" I asked him. "No," he replied with a level gaze, "but it sounds like you have. I am the architect ..." Not a pleasant moment. He was gracious, but it was awkward.

And it's important to keep perspective. Any venue can work if you really want it to. I met a woman recently who spent years sheltering from the bombing in Sarajevo and emerged having taught herself fluent English by the light of a flashlight. If she can do that, we can certainly make a neon-lit, airless cubbyhole work for the occasional meeting if we have to. The key is to be conscious of our surroundings, however supportive or distracting, and be aware of the effect that is having on us.

Sometimes you can even use discomfort to creative effect. I remember watching the CEO of a German telecoms company conscientiously setting up his meeting room on the evening before a conference was to begin. He was creating a perfect, dare I say Teutonically perfect, horseshoe of chairs so that all members of his executive team could see the screen. The theme of the meeting was to be taking on new markets, and his intent was to fire up his board so they would have the courage and daring to step out of the comfort zones of their home territories. When he had gone to the bar I surreptitiously moved the chairs, and the following morning a third of the participants had to lean and peer uncomfortably sideways to see the slides. After a good hour of this suffering I stepped in.

"I notice you guys don't look that comfortable. Is there a problem?"

"Yes," says a spokesperson irritably, "the screen is in the wrong position and we can't see the slides." (The CEO is meanwhile checking his calculations.)

"So why didn't you move it?"

The point wasn't lost on them. You are not going to get anywhere as a company if you don't dare to move from your current position.

This phenomenon of accepting what you are given runs deep in the Anglo-Saxon mentality and, I suggest, in the north of Europe generally. I don't know if it's a hangover from post-war austerity (you'll eat what you are given), but generally people seem to make do with what they are presented with (as individuals and as businesses) because it seems, well, rude to ask for more.

North Americans are better at expressing their needs (as all those self-help books tell them to), but even they are not immune. I was recently playing Meeting Doctor to a top team in Philadelphia. The top team, so the logic goes, gets the top floor and a very swish one at that, with a breathtaking view over the historic city. But I was feeling impish that morning, and as an experiment I lowered the computer-controlled sunblinds so the room was plunged into semi-darkness. The team entered, bumped around a bit and then plowed into the meeting. I swear this group of high-flyers would have sat in the twilight for the entire morning if I hadn't asked them to pause and reflect on how well the meeting was going. They did eventually admit it was a little gloomy. "So why don't you change it? It's *your* meeting room." After a pause someone did get up and raise the blinds, bathing the room in dazzling sunlight.

It puzzled me then and puzzles me still that people would rather suffer a poor environment than act to improve it. OK, it may seem a bit confrontational to ask restaurants to turn down or change music that is irritating you—which I do constantly, to the endless embarassment of my family. But isn't it even odder when the owners of the building themselves don't feel they can open a curtain? Is it because they don't feel it's their place to (even though it quite literally is)? Or maybe it is that we are so focused on what is going on in our heads that we have ceased to register what is going on around us. I fear this is often the root cause.

School has a lot to answer for in this regard. I remember my own classroom was manifestly set up to immobilize children. The assumption seems to be that you can either move *or* think; that suppressing physical activity increases mental activity. Actually, rather than competing, all the evidence suggests that these two activities support each other.

Move It!

We are three-, not two-dimensional beings. We live in space, we express ourselves in movement. It is a woefully outmoded idea that thinking only happens in the head. Your brain is connected through the brain stem to the spine, and thence to an awe-inspiring network of pathways throughout the body. Intelligence is distributed. Though your cerebellum might not like the idea, your knees, ankles, elbows, fingers, and wrists have a wisdom of their own.

I had a vivid recent experience of how the brain can be totally out of step with the body when my cycle-loving accountant, Laurence, persuaded me to ride from London to Brighton, on England's south coast, to help raise money for a local charity. I should explain I am not from what you'd call a sports background. "Contact sport" in our family meant a vigorous game of chess. So when I found myself sitting on a hard bicycle saddle with 60 miles of winding roads ahead of me, my mind was full of misgivings. "You're not fit enough!" "You're not naturally physical!" "You must be mad!" The mental commentary was continuous— and very unhelpful. Until I actually started pedaling. In no time my mind was silenced as the body took over. With very little help from my intellect, the body seemed to know just what to do. My knees pumped away merrily and, as the miles disappeared, it felt as though my body was taking my brain for a ride. By the time we arrived at the seaside, my brain had caught up and was congratulating itself with new beliefs about my extraordinary athletic prowess. But the truth is, it was a day when my doing completely outperformed my thinking.

We have to relearn the lessons of previous cultures and remember past wisdom. Ancient traditions have both sitting meditations and walking meditations. It is said that Aristotle (father of peripatetic teaching) used to conduct lectures on foot, understanding that movement aids the thinking process. Shamans go on physical as well as imagined journeys to solve problems. Sufis dance and twirl themselves into higher states of awareness. Archimedes, let us not forget, had his eureka moment not slogging away at work, but when he broke the pattern of intense thinking and slipped into his bath. Newton had his famous moment of genius after seeing a physical apple physically dropping to earth. Time and time again physical action precedes, or is a component of, an intellectual breakthrough.

Anyone with children will see how moving is central to their imagination. Only last week my daughter Elsa was "stuck" trying to write a story. She was stuck in both senses, physically as well as mentally—hunkered down in her chair as if welded to it, and massaging her head as if physically trying to extrude some ideas from her brainbox. Only because I have been there myself, I suggested we walk around the backyard and talk about the story. We began to move and the ideas began to flow again.

In a very similar way Hollywood writers (who often write in pairs) are seen walking around the lot gesticulating as they tease out a script problem. This works because:

> *any change of physical state tends to change your mental state*
> *your body has intelligence that you are not accessing if you are sitting still*

For the brain, the real and imagined are much closer than we might think—and physically advancing (walking forward) seems to get the brain advancing too. Often you'll find ideas don't get "thought," they simply appear, as landscape might reveal itself on an actual walk.

Freeing your limbs to move also liberates the intelligence within them. There is a child inside us who has not grown up and knows that new ideas—just like the purple dragon we conjured out of air—are sometimes better physically described than written down.

Just as our schoolrooms were mechanisms of restraint, so too are our offices and meeting rooms. The occasional bean bag aside, the standard issue work equipment is still a chair and a desk (as it was at school) and a PC. We automatically talk about "sitting down and working things out," By sitting scrunched at your desk massaging your brows you are proclaiming to the world, "Look how hard I am working!" You can imagine a hunter-gatherer ancestor beamed in from some primeval forest thinking, "Why is this person doing nothing?"

It is true that our work has in many senses been migrating inward, from physical toil to less muscular activities like thinking, problem solving, playing online poker when no one is watching. But we are in danger of taking things too far and immobilizing ourselves completely—which does not help our thinking.

Nor is it great for our body. We may not be hefting rocks or operating heavy machinery, but sitting still is exacting just as heavy a toll on our poor backs and necks.

One person slumped in a chair trying to think clever thoughts is sad enough. But the effect is exponentially increased when you have a whole meeting doing this together. Energy is contagious. But so is sloth. Enervation spreads in a meeting, whether it's across a room or over a phone line.

When you feel yourself drifting it usually means you are lost somewhere in your mind. Even simple movements like wiggling your toes can be enough to break the pattern and bring you back to presence. Better still, get up and move around. Many people ask us for "energizers" to help jump-start fading meetings. Often simply breaking the pattern of behavior (a pattern-interrupt as the NLP world would have it) is sufficient to put color back into the cheeks.

The advice I give for meetings is simply:

> *If you get stuck, move!*
> *If you need some inspiration, breathe!*

Break the Pattern, Challenge the Convention

One way to break the pattern is to challenge meeting conventions. The simplest changes can make a huge difference.

One of our clients, Dell, were holding an offsite meeting championing the idea that every customer is different and needs a customized computer. To make the point we convinced the hotel to dispense with the rows of identical, velour-covered conference chairs and instead imported 312 completely different seats for the delegates. They included a throne, tennis umpire's chair, milking stool, inflatable sofa, swings, you name it ... Not only did delegates get the commercial message of the conference, but they hurried back from breaks to nab the coolest chairs.

All Aboard-room!

I like to ask business audiences how they would ideally allocate their time between the following three activities: work, play, and work-play (a hybrid of the two). The outright winner wherever I ask this question is the work-play category. People the world over would, if they could, spend the lion's share of their time on work that felt like play—playful productivity, if you like.

Co-working entrepreneur Tom Ball was at a bachelor party when he had what I think of as a classic work/play idea. "The party was a bit awkward at first with a lot of guys standing around trying to get to know one another. What they didn't know was that I had organized a rock and roll tour bus to take us all on a mystery tour. The minute we got on board, all the barriers came down. We were off on a shared journey. I was wondering how this could be applied to business when I saw a bus for sale. We bought it and converted it into a fully equipped mobile boardroom (www.allaboardroom.com). Teams love it. They can get away from the office without leaving the office. The offsite spirit begins the minute they get on board."

As Tom adds: "It's a boardroom, not a bored room."

Take a Break from the Breaks

It may seem a small detail, but why not rethink the refreshments offered during the day? Replace the cookies and soda with bottled or filtered water and dried fruit, oat bars, and other foods which build energy, rather than overloading participants with nerve-frazzling, adrenalin-sapping, anxiety-boosting sugars and e-numbers. Dosing a business team with caffeine and glucose is a little like feeding sweets to a car full of toddlers. Hyperactivity followed by a sugar crash. I'd estimate that this simple change can add 20 percent effectiveness to the day. And forget the coffee break—have food available throughout the day, so people can graze rather than have to break a meeting just when it is getting interesting because—da daa!—the donuts have arrived.

Get Fit ...

Hotels increasingly offer health facilities. But why stop there? At a recent business retreat we issued everyone with a pedometer that recorded every step they took during the event. We added these up periodically and plotted the group's progress as though they were on a sponsored walk around the country. It's amazing how far a group of 40 people collectively walk in a normal retreat. The competitive spirit kicked in, with participants starting to take the stairs rather than elevators. One jogger was found with several of his colleagues' pedometers strapped to him. Illegal but ingenious. And a deserving charity finally benefited when the company donated real money for every virtual mile walked.

Or Get Out

Meeting rooms are often buried inside or, in the case of many hotels, underneath buildings. People sit round a table facing into the center of the room, with their backs turned to the frosted glass panels and windows. Is it any wonder meetings become a little inward-looking?

When my teams want to discuss the outside world, I suggest they hold the meeting there. In hotel lobbies, the bed department of a local superstore, on a train, in the street ... Anywhere but a meeting room.

The Twin Room Approach

In the mid-nineties we were working with a part of Ericsson's business that wanted to change how they were perceived by their customers. They had been known as a "box-seller" providing clients with hardware and now wanted to be seen as a more holistic service helping clients solve business problems. This was going to require significant changes in how their people thought about their business. And just as importantly, how they acted. In designing a key meeting that would embrace both the intellectual and operational, we used a simple device of conducting the meeting in two adjacent meeting spaces with a connecting door in between. One was set up as a business forum, the other was an open activity space. We did the "head" stuff in one and then changed rooms to "put the ideas on their feet." The participants shuttled between those two rooms for three days; constantly swapping from the world of Thought to the world of Action and back again. By the end of the second day, the participants were calling for a third room which would integrate both worlds— precisely the message of the meeting—so we simply rolled back the dividing wall and held the final day in a big, unified space.

Putting different dimensions in different rooms is a simple technique that works very well even if you have modest resources of space.

And My Dream Item?

If you are thinking about equipping any meeting room, it's a good idea to get chairs that swivel and roll. Suddenly you have multiplied the possible set-ups you can achieve with minimum sweat. You also reduce significantly the neck strain on your colleagues, who would otherwise spend whole days craning their necks, like a cabbie, to see both you and the screen in what I call Café Style Conference Whiplash.

There are two other pieces of meeting furniture which I'd include every time if I had my way. One is the meeting table that converts into a piano. They have one at the Hub, a fantastic co-working site I often visit in Amsterdam. This nicely combines work with the Dutch concept of Gezellig, which is untranslatable but the nearest we have in English is "homeyness." There is a sense, especially in the Hub, that work is best conducted in a warm, friendly atmosphere where a rousing song is just a flick of a switch away.

In summary, what happens around the meeting is as important as what happens in it. An effective meeting lives in a particular space and time. Acknowledge the bigger picture. Use whatever your environment offers you.

Getting the Best from Virtual Meetings

Before we complete our journey around the real meeting model with a visit to Content, let's spend a moment talking about Virtual Meetings.

First, take a stretch, a walk around the building, kick the cat and/or grab a glass of water. Virtual meetings need more energy and attention than most people realize.

Back? Feeling perky? OK.

Having been provocative earlier in the book about the perils of technology-enabled "fake meetings," I want to take a look at how we can get the most out of these new media.

Business continues to globalize and companies continue to expand geographically. At the same time there are growing concerns about the financial and environmental impact of jumping into cars and onto planes for meetings. No wonder Virtual Meeting technology is constantly evolving new ways of connecting us without physically meeting.

Instant Messaging, PDAs, tele-, video-, and web-conferencing, Wikis, Collaboration Technology, Unified Comms, Presence ... The list of connective technology grows by the day. By the time you are reading this book, they may be trying to beam PowerPoint directly onto your retina ...

As anyone who uses, or is experimenting with any of these technologies will tell you—they all have their strengths and weaknesses.

We do whole programs to help clients master these new media, and there isn't space here to cover all the detail. So what I'd like to offer you here are a few basic principles that will work across the board.

Everything Changes, Nothing Changes

The first thing I'd say is nothing about these media changes the basic fundamentals of meeting. The same rules apply—only more so.

Easier equals Harder

Labor-saving devices have an annoying way of making us busier. Think about all the time you spend scrubbing that high-speed Juice Maker to remove all bits of orange pulp. Because email is much *less* labor intensive than writing a letter, we write vastly *more* of them, and all the time we would have saved is spent managing our bulging, digital in-trays.

Technology now increases the number of people we can contact, but that multiplies the demand on us to communicate well. The danger of a misplaced word or an embarrassing oversight is now hugely amplified.

Broadcasting requires Broadcasters

Because of this amplifying effect I recommend clients think of virtual meeting technology as *broadcast* rather than *communication*.

The modern human spends a huge amount of time watching TV shows and movies which have been expertly produced with big budgets and realer-than-life Special Effects. We have become expert consumers of media. Our eyes and ears pick up *everything*. We have high expectations and are easily disappointed. Remember this when you are setting up a tele- or web-conference. It used to be that only Captains of Industry needed media training. Now media is everywhere. We are all broadcasting (YouTube's strapline is, let's remember, *Broadcast Yourself*) and we would do well to up our game.

Yes, I know you think you have the natural charisma of a George Clooney or Meryl Streep and that it's just going to flood through the webcam effortlessly. The truth is that George and Meryl work hard at their craft to make it look natural—and so should you.

Set the Stage

Context is more important than ever here. Participants in a teleconference are flying "blind," deprived of all senses except that of hearing. For the exchange to be meaningful it is essential people understand where they are, who is there with them, and where they are going. Radio announcers, newscasters, and DJs are masters of this, gently taking the listeners by the hand and keeping them oriented on the sound journey.

> *"...Thank you Mr. John Nutt. That was the Senator giving his view on the recent transportation crisis. We are going now for a reaction from Mrs. Genevieve Bolt, mayor of the town that stands in the path of the giant new highway. But before we speak to her, remember we want to hear your views and you can share them by calling us now on 123 4567."*

In our virtual meeting trainings we actively encourage clients to practice running teleconferences like a radio-phone in. You'd be amazed how it boosts the energy of even a routine call when you imagine the public is listening in. Whenever I have done radio interviews myself or recorded music performances I am amazed how the red "LIVE" light sends my own pulse racing. It may sound like a cozy conversation with the presenter, but inside I am at 110 percent concentration. The opportunity of communicating to millions of people—and the possibility of messing up in front of them—concentrates the mind wonderfully! This energy can be harnessed to make an ordinary conference call really fizz.

Lead the Call

If leadership is important in a face-to-face meeting, it's vital in a virtual one. If you have more than two participants, especially in different time zones, someone has to lead. If not it will be a waste of time and you might as well hang up.

People may protest at this extra layer of structure. "Why complicate things?" they'll ask. "Why can't we just talk in a natural organic, self-organizing way?" You can, but imagine, if you will, a busy airport that decided to let the incoming and outgoing flights self-organize. It would be beautifully organic. It would also be carnage.

Think of virtual meeting leadership like Air Traffic Control orchestrating proceedings (or "Voice Traffic Control" as my colleague Michelle puts it).

Speaking from experience as an amateur pilot, you can feel "blind" flying up there and it's massively reassuring to hear the voice of the Air Traffic Controller telling you your precise position and alerting you to the aircraft in front, behind, above, and below you. It's very un-aviation to gush, but I swear I could have kissed the superb professional who received a panicked call from me one morning. With the weather souring and fuel on the low side, I was looking desperately for Oxford Airport. The map said I was in the right position. So did the GPS. But I just couldn't see it anywhere. "Charlie Bravo, I believe we are underneath you" said the cheerful ATC without a hint of sarcasm. "Try looking down." Whoever you are, thanks for not treating me with the derision I deserved.

Bottom line: a leaderless tele- or video-conference is like heavy traffic on a slick road in heavy fog. Without clear direction you are headed for either a long wait, stressful gridlock, or a painful pile-up.

The Audience Sees and Hears EVERYTHING

Video-conferencing and its fancy Hi-Definition big brother, Telepresence, are a bid to make the interface between participants in a remote meeting as real as possible. One client I know has Virtual Presence suites where their board table has been halved and ends at a wall-sized screen, where it is completed by the image of its partner half somewhere on the other side of the world. This is a nice visual device to enhance the feeling that the two sets of participants are in the same space and time. You feel you can reach out and touch the spots on your colleague's tie half-way round the world. The trouble is, *everything* is in vivid Technicolor. If someone loses attention and stifles a yawn, you see it. If someone's eyelids droop or they "secretly" consult their BlackBerry, you see it. Thanks to the amplifying effect of broadcast, everything is seen—even more clearly than it would be live.

A famous study (by the University of Hertfordshire in the 1990s) showed that radio listeners pick up lies quicker and more accurately than TV viewers. There is apparently something about closing down one sense (sight) that makes the other (hearing) sharper and more acute. So beware. You may think that people do not sense your inattention on a phone call when you are doodling or answering emails, but they do. If you are on the phone, imagine people can see what you are doing and act accordingly.

Another way to describe this is ...

Don't Hide behind the Medium

We've all had the experience of shouting angrily at another motorist from the security of your moving vehicle—only to draw up beside them at the lights and feel thoroughly abashed. It's amazing how rude we can be at a distance. And how that boldness evaporates when the contact is face to face. If you wouldn't say it to their face, don't say it on the phone.

Lights, Camera, Action

I belong to a business club in London where the other members have become quite used to me wandering around looking for a place with the right light and background noise level for a Skype video call.

Maybe it's my theater training (or vanity), but speaking to a client that can't see or hear me seems counterproductive.

The right height is important, too. Put your laptop on a normal table and, thanks to the webcam angle, the other person finds themselves looking right up your nose. I wasn't aware of this until David, my own performance coach, pointed out the effect made him feel like "a spider in a tea cup." The effect is easily cured by putting your laptop on a couple of books to raise the screen.

And here's another off-putting, connection-killing habit to watch out for. Imagine you are trying to tell a colleague something important and they refuse to meet your eye. It would certainly cramp my style. Yet that's precisely the effect you give when you spend your time looking at the screen image rather than right into your webcam.

Until they put laptop webcams in the middle of the screen—like a teleprompter—see if you can concentrate on speaking "into the camera," so the people you are speaking to don't have the uncomfortable feeling that you are avoiding their gaze.

Really Listen

A telephone conversation should make listening easier, but for some reason it doesn't. How many times have you put down the phone and wondered, what did she/he say? Even with detailed notes it is easy to misunderstand or mis-communicate.

A great way to illustrate this is an exercise created by my friend the mischievous NLPer Michael Breen called "Martian Tea Party." In it colleague A (Earthling) instructs colleague B (Martian) how to make a cup of tea by giving instructions over the phone. It's colleague B's first visit to Earth. He has no knowledge of the unfamiliar apparatus in front of him (teapot, tea bag, kettle, hot water, spoon) so relies entirely on what he hears. He only knows he has to follow the instructions he hears *literally* and *to the letter*. Teapots are mistaken for cups, the kettle stays cold because no one told anyone to turn it on, spoons are used upside down, water goes everywhere ... It's an amusing but instructive demonstration of how hard it is to communicate clearly purely through the medium of voice and language. Bring towels ...

A good question to ask yourself is: *Am I listening to what they are saying, or to what I think they are saying*? While we are talking on the phone, our minds are having a parallel conversation, interpreting, judging, filtering, and sorting the information. This inner conversation is often easier to remember than the actual one. It's a good idea to check by asking, "This is what I think I heard you say, am I right?"

What's more, successful listening on the phone requires hearing not just what is said but what is *not* said. If you want to get expert in the medium, listen out for who hasn't contributed and encourage them to speak. Also, start sensing when someone wants to say more and needs to be coaxed and encouraged to do so.

Two short better than one long

Given the concentration that virtual meetings require, it is easy to get tired and lose focus. It's far better to break the meetings into smaller chunks than go for a marathon which is beyond our stamina to complete successfully.

If we start thinking like radio broadcasters, we realize that the ad break, weather report, and news update are all ways to give the listener a moment to pause and refresh their ability to listen.

A prop I like to use in live client meetings is a bell, the sort you see on the counter in traditional hotels. This bell gets "ping-ed" every 20 minutes (about as long as most of us ordinary humans can sustain attention) to remind participants that time is passing and giving everyone a small moment to hit their own re-boot button.

You can have similar "ping" moments in a virtual meeting. If you are using a system that incorporates the ability to see slides, then I find a brightly colored slide reading PING! does the trick.

There is only one real Broadband

As impressive as technology is becoming, however fat your data pipe or gushy your bit torrent rate, none of it compares with the richness of information the human mind can "upload" at dizzying speed in a live meeting.

I may have to eat my words when a 3D holographic tele-porter comes out next year. Till then, I'd say there is no substitute for face-to-face interaction, especially when the stakes are high.

As Oxfam's Dame Barbara Stocking puts it succinctly: "You can do telephone and video conferences, but these only work well if you have met before—particularly if the issue is serious. Once you have had a good-quality face-to-face meeting you can then work with virtual media."

Social philosopher and writer Charles Handy echoes this point: "On the phone people are just disembodied voices. Video can help, but even so ... If you want to make real contact with people, get their legs under your table." He and his photographer wife Liz have taken these words literally and for many years have been inviting people to their London home for their now legendary breakfasts. I am one of probably hundreds of people who have sat with their knees under the Handy kitchen table talking about future plans and dreams.

"Liz makes sure people come with a project idea or issue in mind," says Charles. "They know they have one hour exactly. It's a special opportunity to do some thinking. What we do, if we can restrain ourselves, is simply to listen. And if our guests have questions they can then generally tell themselves their own answers."

Why breakfast in a kitchen and not a Skype call? "We feel it's a special place. It creates an intimacy. You leave on first-name terms."

In this time- and cost-conscious world, you don't always have the luxury of getting "knees under the table" for a face-to-face meeting. Real meeting is becoming a very valuable commodity. That's all the more reason to make sure you get real value from it.

Content

The What of Meetings

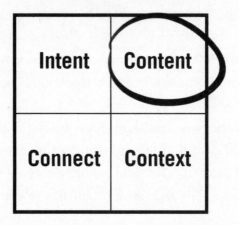

Meetings are too full and the content is often irrelevant. The secret is to stop *assembling* and start *designing the content* of your meetings. We are going to end our whistlestop tour through the anatomy of a meeting where most people start—and spend most of their time. On content.

In a world that's complex, emergent, and fuzzy, it's totally understandable that we are drawn to things you can write down, print out, and hold in your hand. Like the agenda of meeting. Weeks in advance, sometimes months (in the case of quarterly or annual meetings) we will sit down and solemnly work out what should go into a meeting.

Typically meetings are built on the foundation of content. Context may be mentioned—and the invitation list given the once-over. Intent rarely if ever gets a look in. And the result, as we are seeing, is meetings that are content-rich/intent-poor, long on the *what* and short on the *why*.

If the meeting is a large or important one, the agenda develops into a running order or "script" many sheets (and sometimes inches) deep where every imagined scrap of content is included, timed and systematically ordered. This is where you'll see *11.17–11.22 cookies (inc. gluten free)* to be served and *10.14 bio break*.

Beware the Kebab Syndrome

This is what I call the *kebab syndrome*. On the three sunny days we experience in the UK every year, normally undomesticated males dust off their barbeques and take charge of the cooking. They bring together a variety of meats, vegetables (and the occasional pineapple chunk), and ram these on to skewers, usually too many and too close to cook well. Following a Trial by Fire (or in reality charcoal briquettes, lighter fluid, and finally gasoline) the partially cooked and mostly burned kebabs emerge to be eaten though not necessarily digested. Not a pretty analogy for how we put meetings together, but a valid one. Chunks of material are forced together into too small a space, under-processed and poorly assimilated. It's the difference between design and assembly. A great meeting, like a great meal, is designed. Fast food is assembled. A Rolls-Royce is designed from the chassis up. A Trabant is assembled from a store of available ingredients.

Think of the integral anatomy we have been exploring as your guide to designing rather than assembling meetings.

Agendas, Scripts, and Scenarios

Agenda means literally "the things to be done." It is effectively a to-do list, a sequence of actions that you are planning to take during a meeting.

I don't know if you are a fan of to-do lists, but I am not. I tend to put too much on mine. I don't order them well. There are always more items unchecked than checked. And they are endless. It is much easier to put things on than take them off.

By the way, a good exercise here is to ask your team/colleagues/reports to write down their top ten priorities. Then have them cross out all but the top three and concentrate on them. (Three is about all we can handle ...)

Don't get me wrong, I think checklists have their place. As an amateur pilot, for example, I have come to rely on the meticulous pre-flight checklists that are designed to make sure you don't take off with, for example, your fuel cap loose. I only mention this because the one time I thought I would dispense with the checklist that is precisely what I did. If you do that in a car, the results can be costly, spraying expensive gasoline all over the highway. If you do it in a plane, the outcome can be a lot more serious—and messy.

When it comes to meetings, though, I suggest we think "scenario" rather than "agenda."

To explain the difference, let me take you to a street in Medieval Italy where a group of street comics are doing a show to a rowdy lunchtime audience. This is a *commedia dell'arte* troupe, featuring characters like Harlequin, Columbine, and Pulcinella (or Punch, of Punch and Judy fame). They make their living traveling from town to town, improvising raucously funny and often libelous shows. Or appearing to improvise. In fact what these seasoned performers are doing is improvising around a basic template. They have hundreds in their repertoire and to remind them which they are doing today, they tack a piece of paper with the basic outline on to the scenery—hence "scenario." Now that everyone knows the basic shape, length, and direction of the show, they can improvise confidently within this agreed structure.

A scenario is what I recommend my clients create to guide them through a meeting. It must fit on one side of a sheet of paper at most. Ideally, I try to get my own scenarios onto the back of a movie ticket. It's a great discipline.

A scenario. Not an agenda. And most definitely not a script.

Unlike the single-sheet scenario, a script is a thick, spiral-bound document containing comprehensive details of what should be said and done at each and every moment of the play.

What our meetings need is a scenario. What they often have is a script.

Films need scripts. Life does do not. *The Truman Show* gave a comic glimpse of what life might be like if it were minutely scripted—if all the spontaneity and trivial detail was actually minutely planned. Though he is unaware of it, Truman (Jim Carrey) is actually the subject of a virtual reality TV show watched by millions and presided over by godlike director Ed Harris, who is orchestrating everything, including the weather, from his studio in the sky.

It's a nightmarish vision, but there's something in it that attracts us. Especially when we plan events like meetings. Inside us lurks that omnipotent director with a megaphone who wants to control everything that is going to happen.

And if the meeting is an important one, this process can begin months before the meeting actually takes place. You could call it competent planning. What I more often see is a desire to remove the risk of the unknown. Structure, the thinking goes, creates stability. If we structure the future, we can control it.

The result is wildly detailed running orders for meetings (with those cookies at 11.17 ...) that have taken hours to create and generally kill the aliveness of the meeting when it actually arrives. Imagine you were on a date and your partner kept checking a script to see what was supposed to happen next ... You get the idea.

The balance between structure and freedom is a delicate one—clearly you need both—and every meeting designer/leader has to find their own equilibrium.

If it is a script you want, then do remember that even Shakespeare's scripts indicate only what is to be said by which character in what setting. The script has to be brought to life through a live experience.

When you sit down (or walk around) to plan a meeting, I'd suggest there are three clear options to choose from:

> *Fully scripted*
> *Fully improvised*
> *Part scripted/part improvised*

Fully Scripted

It has become common practice to fully script large-scale meetings such as Shareholder Presentations, All Staff Sales Kick Offs, etc. I personally think they feel a bit like the Oscars—artificial reality. All the jokes are pre-rehearsed, the emotion is on tap, the comfort breaks timed to fit the advertising slots. Clearly, when there are lots of moving parts it is important to have a common script for all parties to read off, but do see if you can puncture the structure with some un- or semi-scripted breathing holes.

Fully Improvised

This is truly what most of our meetings are, particularly when we turn up ad hoc unprepared for a meeting without knowing who else will be there and why.

In improv circles we have a game called "Thank God You Are Here," where a performer walks unprepared into a cocktail party of pre-briefed colleagues and has to guess from the reactions of the other guests who she is and what she does.

Humans are good at improvising. We have been doing it all our lives. I sometimes want to remind people of this when they turn up at our show and find the whole idea of speaking without any script quite a daunting and dazzling concept.

The problem (or virtue) of true improvisation is that you never quite know where you are going to end up.

A golden rule of theatrical improv is that you say "yes" to whatever happens and build upon it. If someone introduces the subject of Victorian Fashion, or 1980s Songs, or Dinosaur Dentists, your job as an improviser is to accept and develop that theme. This can be very entertaining for improv shows, but it's murder for meetings. You start talking about Sales Targets. This morphs seamlessly into a Chat About Personnel then on to a quick Gossip About Steve and ends with a Moan About IT.

Part Scripted/Part Improvised

For most meetings there is a mid-point between these two extremes—the over-rigid and the dangerously wobbly—where you create enough structure to insure the meeting has clear direction, and enough freedom for the meeting to breathe. It's the approach that is used for most chat shows or discussion programmes on radio or television.

There are those who say the key to a great meeting is to create an agenda and follow it. I say create an agenda and then follow WHAT IS HAPPENING. If you have your head stuck in the agenda instead of what is going on in the room you're like a skier hurtling down a mountain while reading the How to Ski book.

The broadcaster Jonathan Miller was once interviewing the great violinist David Oistrakh, asking which was more important—the notes (created by the composer) or the performance (created by the performer). Oistrakh tossed a Beethoven score onto the piano, cupped his ear and said, with a grin, "I don't hear anything ..." He was pointing out that, no matter how great the score, the notes printed on the paper, it needs to be performed if it is to come to life. Think of your agenda as notes that have to be performed and you won't go far wrong.

Fearless Meeting Design

The ability to imagine vividly an event in the future is a wonderful and, I believe, peculiarly human gift. Yes, there are animals that can "imagine" beyond the present to anticipate future events, but few of them could plan a surprise birthday party.

I had never really thought about this until a friend of mine, William Kendall, a superb business mind and very commercially inventive fellow, asked me to help him plan his wedding service. William can slice and dice a profit and loss spreadsheet in a single glance but was having trouble visualizing the possibilities for his wedding celebration. I started laying out some options for him— this music could go here and these people could stand there— when he stopped me. "You can see this, can't you?" he asked. Partly, I suppose, from my background in theater, and partly through practice, I was indeed "seeing" the event unfold in different ways from different angles in my "mind's eye." Projecting future possibilities onto the screen of your mind is certainly a very helpful faculty to develop when you are planning meetings.

But we have to be careful to not confuse what we "see should happen" with what actually does happen. When we project, speaking in the mental sense rather than cinematic, we tend to project hopes and fears onto future events. We can be too pessimistic, or too exuberantly confident. You can guess which is most common in business.

Pessimism shows up in what I call *fear-driven design*. This is where the decisions you make in advance are based on the assumption that "they" will hate the meeting, or you, or both.

This kind of thinking gives rise to really safe meeting planning as one creative idea after another is dismissed because "they'll never do that" or "it won't work," or a host of other excuses we make, basically to keep ourselves safe and reduce the risk.

Entertainers suffer a lot from this. The more they crave the acceptance of the audience, the more they fear its disapproval.

Use Fear as Fuel

If you do have to fear something, fear being middle-of-the-road in your design choices. Let that fear fuel you to do something different.

I was still new to creating experiences for businesses when I learned a truth that has served me well: *the more alpha the male, the quicker he will put on that dress.*

It was a rumbunctious affair designed to promote Commitment in a senior team. For the "team building" section we created a *Commitments*-style R&B band, but we were down one female backing singer. So why not the chairman? "He'll never do it," we were told. "Absolutely no, forget it." But just in case, we had a rather fabulous femme-fatale red ballgown made in the chairman's size—with neat velcro panels to enable quick entry and exit. Suffice to say that the chairman, who understood the event and why it would be valuable for him to lead by example in showing *some commitment*, was in that dress in a flash. Plus earrings.

Fear-based planning keeps you safe. And keeps you predictable. As *Purple Cow* author Seth Godin puts it nicely, *"Safe is the new risky."*

Why is this so important to remember when you are designing content? Because if you think exclusively about what you expect to happen, instead of what is actually happening, you can miss the best parts of the meeting. *And the best bits are often not planned.*

When Wrong is Right

Some years ago I was helping create a meeting for the owner of Dell computers, Michael Dell. One the world's richest men, Dell was planning to visit his U.K. operation to celebrate New Year's. Visits like this tend to throw local offices into a tizzy. Add the fact that this New Year's party was being held in a small suburb of London, on a rainy Wednesday, at a skating rink in mid-November, and you'll get a sense of the challenge. Expectation was sky high. So was the pressure. Events like this in the U.S. are joyous occasions, all whoop-whooping and air-punching, designed to create a community feel amongst the employees. The corporation was looking for similar enthusiasm and energy. This was the U.K., however, where audiences are more inclined to scoff than holler, where a Wimbledon-like smattering of applause is more likely than unbridled enthusiasm.

A whole posse of executives are assigned to the event, and in the days leading up to it their anxiety reaches fever pitch. It all centers on a key moment when Michael is supposed to press a red button, releasing a cascade of balloons and confetti cannons. It's an essential moment in the agenda. It is something that absolutely "must be done." Emails torrent back and forth between the U.K. and Austin, Texas. A laptop is actually flown to Ireland with the script on it. Everything is done to insure that Michael is forewarned and will press the button at the right moment, unleashing the balloons and the adoration of the crowd. Which, of course, he doesn't.

I was there, MC-ing the meeting, when Michael finished his address and ambled off stage at the key moment, without pressing the famous button. At the back of the hall, a whole team of execs were wildly miming button-pushing. Panic. The moment had been missed. Horror. The agenda was not being followed.

In theater you learn, quickly, that when something goes wrong like this it's a huge opportunity. We all know something has gone wrong—we have wandered off script—but the audience is watching to see how you handle it. This is the moment you can either lose them, or win them for life.

The whole idea of this meeting, the intent, was to create community and to do this by giving Dell's U.K. employees the feeling of a direct personal connection with their eponymous boss. Hitherto, the meeting had gone well but was a formal affair, dutifully following the agenda but not lighting any fires. Michael Dell's unexpected exit was an opportunity which I seized without thinking. "Hey, Michael!" I called. "Get back here."

I could feel the breath constrict in a thousand throats. "Did he just call our multimillionaire boss by his *first name*???" For the first time the event really had some excitement. Would the expendable facilitator be skewered? Mr Dell, like many owner-founders I have met, is actually a pretty relaxed guy. He ambled back onstage, where I clasped my arm round his shoulder. There was an audible intake of breath. ("*He touched his suit! He touched his SUIT!*") To be honest I wasn't sure what to do next. I was off script too. But I motioned toward the audience and said in an audible undertone, "Michael, they didn't come here to see me. They came here to see ... YOU." There was a second of silence and then a truly Texas-sized wave of roaring, clapping, and cheering. Though it wasn't planned, this unexpected hiatus, this problem-resolved provided exactly what the event needed. A bit of life, a blast of danger, a taste of the unpredicted. With the pressure valve released, we could return to the agenda. The button was pressed, the balloons dropped, the confetti cannons exploded and the whole place celebrated.

Meetings are like that. Have an agenda by all means—it is important to have an idea of what is going to happen—but pay real attention to what is actually happening. It will be more interesting than anything you plan.

Like most great moments in a meeting, it wasn't planned or scripted. It was a happy accident: one of those moments that initially seems worthless and mundane yet brings true value and insight. It was a moment that everyone there would remember long after the official agenda was forgotten.

Cell Phones On!

Another happy accident that will be long remembered occurred when I was leading an innovation meeting with a large group of committed but harassed government employees.

The subject was "smart working." I wanted to help this group disconnect from their daily routine to find the space and time to look at and think about their goal from a fresh perspective; so we'd brought them far out of their normal environment to The

Ministry of Sound, a huge nightclub in London. The meeting was going well but it was not spectacular—until someone's cell phone rang. Like a school of distracted porpoises, the participants dove on their bags and into their pockets, praying that they weren't the guilty culprits. We've all been there. The professional facilitator in me was about to wait patiently for the blushing owner of the ringing phone to turn it off when it suddenly dawned on me: this was The Moment I had been waiting for.

"Everyone, please turn on your cells," I said. A sea of blank stares. "No, I mean it. Cells on. Everyone. Hold them up above your head and listen." One by one arms went up until there were three hundred hands holding aloft a forest of cell phones. For a minute or so we sat in awkward silence, and then it began.

At first a chirrup, then a beep. Then a digital dawn chorus signaling the arrival of the first wave of text messages and voicemails. This was followed by a rapid crescendo until the room was filled with a deafeningly loud impatient electronic symphony. Laughter erupted, and then it subsided as the moment of humor passed and the real message sank in. This moment, since dubbed the Blizzard, brought home to each of us just how in demand we are all the time. One by one we realized how precious our time is, how obligated we are to other people, and how important it is to switch off the everyday pressures if we are to switch on our creativity.

Strontium and Sweat

In 2011 I found myself tramping through a Redwood forest in northern California with a bunch of free thinkers including the political activist and environmental campaigner Jim Garrison. Jim, a long-time champion of real meeting, offered me this compelling example of what happens when something—or in this case someone—that was never in a script, absolutely transformed a meeting.

Back in 1978, I had been doing a lot of civil disobedience around nuclear power plants, and I ended up in Oklahoma working on the Karen Silkwood case.

I found myself joining up with various activists there, around a nuclear power plant they were building outside of Tulsa, at a place called Black Fox. At that time it was considered to be impossible to stop the Redneck, highly funded oil and nuclear industries in a place like Oklahoma. Nevertheless a few of us met and kind of took up the challenge. We weren't making a huge amount of progress in the meeting when a man stood up and said "I want to introduce you to somebody. He's an old medicine man—a Cherokee."

So we trooped out of the meeting room and reconvened at this venerable medicine man's sweat lodge. We were all taken out of our normal categories of discourse and perception by spending all night looking into a fire, getting up at three o'clock, building the fire for the smoke lodge, and then going through a sweat together. It put us all in such an altered state that we became optimized individuals, and we ended up in very short order—in only about six weeks— mobilizing the largest civil disobedience in the history of the southwest part of the United States. And we ended up stopping that nuclear reactor.

The point I would make here is that meetings often achieve breakthrough when an element that no one expects asserts itself quite dramatically and takes everybody out of their normal reality.

Nicely put, Jim.

Text and Subtext

So when you are designing content you have to plan for the unplanned. Another thing you need to be aware of is that, whether you are using agenda, script, or scenario, the content is not what appears on the page. What is written is a small proportion of the real communication. When you are in a meeting, the delivery of the words is as important as the words themselves. People are picking up not just what is said but also how it's said and who is saying it. The comment of a boss will usually be given different weight to that of a junior. And just as crucial is all the information that is *not said*, but communicated silently through a roll of the eyes, an imperceptible nod or a sideways glance.

This is one of the things that make telephone conference calls a particular challenge. The folks on the phone can't see the non-verbal communication, so we are left with simply words and tonality.

The arts are completely comfortable with the idea that there is *text* (what is said) and *subtext* (what is never said but is nevertheless understood). In drama it's not only not a problem, it's the norm.

You may remember the scene in *Annie Hall* when Woody Allen's character is getting to know Diane Keaton's on the balcony of a New York apartment. While the characters are chatting awkwardly, the subtitles tell us what they are really thinking—the subtext.

SCRIPT	SUBTITLES
He: Did you do those photographs in there, or what?	
She: Yeah, I sort of dabble around	Dabble? Listen to me. What a jerk!
He: They are wonderful. They have a quality	You are a great looking girl
She: I would like to take a serious photography course	He probably thinks I am a yo-yo
He: Photography is interesting as it's a new art form and a set of esthetic criteria has not emerged yet	I wonder what she looks like naked?

I'd love to hold a meeting where we project the subtext up on a wall like this:

"Good morning everyone"
(God, I have a headache)

"Nice to see you"

(What time did we leave the bar?)

"I'm delighted that Janice could make it over from Paris to join
us"

(She doesn't trust me)

But the fact is, people are picking up the subtext anyway.

It's something I like to remind clients about if I see them laboring over the exact wording of a presentation or script. What you are going to say is important. But who you are going to be is vital.

No amount of word crafting, script doctoring or PowerPoint voodoo is going to persuade an audience to take in a message you don't believe yourself. We are all very media literate. We are used to the exposé and the close-up. We spot incongruities immediately. Real and spontaneous beat slick and on-message every time.

Real Conversation

Subtext enriches our life. But it can lead to hidden conflict. On the surface all appears peaceful, but underneath our subtexts are at war.

When this happens in meetings I will often hold up a card which reads: *Time for a Real Conversation*. It's a very useful prop. You might want to stick something like it in your wallet.

It's signaling we've reached a moment to "say what isn't being said" or what I call "drain the bathtub." I encourage people to ask themselves:

> *Am I saying what I mean?*
> *Am I meaning what I say?*
> *Am I saying what needs to be said, or what I think others want to hear?*

It is an effective way of "outing" the subtext, pointing out the gorilla on the fridge or the elephant in the room. Here are some good phrases you can use to get a Real Conversation going:

When you said that, what I felt was ...

Is there anything else you want or need to say on that subject?

Can I play back to you what I think I heard?

What is the conversation that we should really be having?

More often than not, the "opponents" discover they are in what I like to call *Furious Agreement*; that is, they essentially want the same thing, but not in quite the same way. For example, the Head of Research and Head of Marketing both want the business to prosper, but they have different ideas about it and both feel that theirs are the best. It's not very edifying, but it is human nature. And smart leaders know how to harness this, so it becomes healthy competition rather than a fight-to-the-death turf war.

It's about time!

The third aspect of meeting design I wanted us to be aware of is time. One of the problems we have with designing content is our inability to imagine ahead of time how long things will actually take. The timeline all makes perfect sense on paper, but has very little to do with what happens on the day. One of my favourite examples of this is what I call CEO-time.

If you hear the phrase *"then John our CEO will talk for ten minutes about ...,"* you must understand that means ten *CEO minutes*. Like cat years, CEO minutes are different from normal human time. They are not defined by the clock, but by what *feels like a minute* to the CEO. I witnessed an extreme case of this at a summer cocktail party we planned, where the CEO assured us he would "spend a few minutes" (alarm) welcoming his sales managers and sharing "some light-touch personal comments." We could dispense with PowerPoint and there would be no need for chairs as this would be over before we knew it. Fifty minutes and three faintings later he was still going strong. When the third person passed out and hit the deck he suggested we "leave the guy there to recover" as he had one more joke to share. Clearly this is an extreme example, and not all CEOs would be that care-free about the timing or the wellbeing of their audience. But still, be alert about CEO time—and help your CEO to be, too.

At the other end of the spectrum we can be too obsessive about clock-watching. The script says six minutes, so we get anxious if it is seven or ten. We forget that this was our estimate in the first place, based on our own best guess of how the event would go.

How do you stay aware of the passing time, even during an intense meeting? The London-based design consultancy ICO came up with a solution I absolutely love when they were challenged by advertising agency Wieden + Kennedy to find ways "intelligent furniture" could improve the quality of their meetings and "stop time running away from us." ICO's solution was the brilliantly simple TimeTable—a table with ten illuminated panels running down the middle, each representing a tenth of the meeting time. You dial in the required meeting length at the start, and as the time passes, panel lights go out one by one. When the allotted meeting time has elapsed, TimeTable will politely inform attendees, "This meeting is now complete, please leave the room in an orderly fashion." Or, and I love this, you can put it into disco mode and when time's up the table plays a funky disco track as the table lights flash in multi-colored *Saturday Night Fever* sequences. I want one!

Too much Content, too little Time

We are not only unrealistic about how long people will talk for, but also about how much content we can usefully cover in a meeting. Here you want to be really conscious not just of how much you can transmit to the audience, but of how much they can reliably receive. Not to mention assimilate and use.

> "How was yesterday's meeting?"
>
> "Great. Fabulous. A milestone."
>
> "What did you learn?"
>
> "No idea ... I'll check my notes if I can find them."

We don't overfill meetings because we are sadists. Our motives are good and we want people to benefit. We just forget, as we craft our elegant running orders, how we ourselves learn; how much we can absorb from a one-hour presentation; how we get tired and need frequent breaks and time to assimilate what we are hearing. And that listening is tiring.

I can do about 20 minutes before my mind wanders. It's wandering now, I notice. Off for a stretch. Back in a moment.

That's better.

We try and increase the amount of content we can cram in by scheduling earlier and earlier starts. It's getting to seem almost wimpish to start an event at 9 or 9.30.—nowadays 8, 7.30 or even 7 is becoming the norm. Of course, if people do make the heroic effort to be there (after leaving the bar at 3 a.m.) it doesn't mean they are actually functioning.*

Presenteeism is an increasingly common feature of businesses and meetings. The body is in the room, but the mind is elsewhere.

Create a Listening

Good performers, entertainers, orators, and communicators know that before people can hear a message you first have to "create a listening." You have to provide the conditions for information to travel across the space between your mouth and their ears. This is the reason rock stars send out a support act first, why operas and musicals begin with an overture, and TV shows with live studio audiences often use a warm-up artist.

---

* People talk about the hour after lunch being the "graveyard shift." I find it's later in the afternoon, around 4.30 (irrespective of time zone), that I sense the attention of participants leaving the room, like souls departing the undead.

Good ways to create a listening in a meeting include:

> **Stating the intention and context.** *If you do this powerfully, it reminds people why they are there and should have them sitting up.*

> **Checking In.** *Before you start with the business itself, the leader of the meeting asks the participants to share one short piece of information with the rest. Take care not to be intrusive or clichéd. Personally I really dislike the question beloved of facilitators around the globe: "Can you tell us one thing that no one knows about you?" Questions that I find do work well include: "Where is your attention at the moment?" ... "What's the most pressing issue you are facing?" ... "On a scale of one to ten, how positive are you about the business at the moment?" ... "What one topic in the national news is on your mind?" If I feel the group's attention seriously needs focusing I sometimes ask a provocative question like: "What percentage of your attention do you intend to bring to the issue we are about to discuss?" If people are disengaged, at least you will know in advance.*

> **Positive Gossip.** *Spend five minutes chatting about the things that are going well. That really takes people by surprise and warms up the connections between them.*

> **Sneak Preview.** *Like a movie trailer, you can give people a foretaste of the content that lies ahead so they can orient themselves.*

> **Humor.** *It's the oldest trick in the book—and don't do it if it seems hackneyed—but making people laugh is a fine way to*

prepare them for collaboration. My mate, the entrepreneur Oli Barrett, is famous for bringing people together. Wired *magazine called him "the most connected man in Britain." He has such passion for connecting people it's become his business (The Co-sponsorship Agency)—or one of them. "I love to start things," he explains, chuckling. "Companies, campaigns, charities ... and meetings." For Oli, the key to a successful meeting is "not starting the business of the meeting before people are really connected. This is why one of my favorite things at the start of the meeting is to get people to do some 'mucking about'. I don't mean getting out clown noses or doing ridiculous games, just a few lighthearted minutes which allow people to relax, launch, and show each other what they are really like. I don't care if I'm in a top corporate boardroom or with the Prime Minister, 'mucking about' is a wonderful way to get a sense of who the other people are, where they come from, create connections and put some energy out there. I find the most senior people, all the way up to chairmen and government ministers, absolutely get this. They really value the moments when the pomposity is punctured. This is why I pepper meetings I am designing with MABs (mucking about breaks). Much more important than AOBs (any other business)."*

> **Silence.** *One of the most powerful things you can say to start a meeting is ... nothing. Silence has become a rare commodity in our busy days and noisy lives. A few moments of silence can be a disarmingly simple way to start a meeting, giving us all time to tune out the background static and start hearing what we really think.*

The Quakers have been onto this for centuries, seeing meetings as essentially silent gatherings where you only speak when you are inspired to say something. Sometimes, as the 90s rock ballad reminds us "You say it best, when you say nothing at all."

All of these techniques, in their way, allow the participants to remember where they are (and why), connect with the other people in the meeting, and warm up the muscles they need to communicate and listen.

The key as a meeting designer is to discount a portion at the head of the meeting and anticipate a tailing off at the end. What's left between these bookends is the useful part of the meeting, the golden zone where useful work can be done.

Designing Real Meetings:
How Long Is a Meeting Hour?

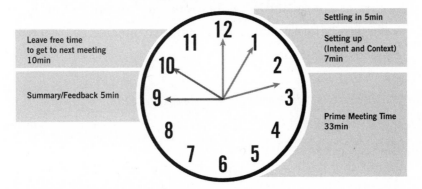

Leave free time to get to next meeting 10min

Summary/Feedback 5min

Settling in 5min

Setting up (Intent and Context) 7min

Prime Meeting Time 33min

Two Golden Rules of Meeting Design

Finally, for when you are designing your meeting content, I'd like to pass on to you a couple of golden rules which have served me well.

Do live what's best done live

Meetings represent a significant expenditure of resources. They are a rare chance to interact live (face to face or voice to voice). Make the most of the opportunity by using that valuable time only for *what can be best done live*. Anything that can be better achieved through a different medium or outside the meeting should not be part of your content. Get rid of it.

Create extraordinary value

There is a second way of filtering possible content that, if you take it on, can revolutionize not only your meetings but your leadership. Before deciding what content to include, ask yourself the following question:

> *"How can this meeting generate extraordinary value for those attending?"*

Asking this shifts you from thinking about input (what we pump into the meeting and its participants) to output (what it would be most valuable for the participants to take out, or do as a result of this meeting). And from process (who says what to whom and when) to value (how this materially advances our business).

Focusing on value-generation has all sorts of benefits. It keeps us sharp, forces us to ask the difficult questions, reminds us why we are there, connects us to our colleagues, and helps us make content decisions on more than personal preference and taste. It's a standard others can and will respect. And if your meeting really does create extraordinary value for those attending, you can bet they will come back—on time—when you need them next.

Most businesspeople see the logic of this switch in attitude but they often struggle to make it. They are so used to thinking, "This is what X needs to hear"—they have forgotten why it's valuable for X to hear it. It is servant leadership in action and is definitely worth a try.

How would you know what would create value for the participants? Ask them! At the end of meetings it is a great practice to canvass participants about what was most valuable for them. It is a very good guide to what people want and need from their meetings. Common sense argues that the more they get this— and only this—the better, more purposeful and probably shorter your meetings will be.

4

THE SEVEN BASIC MEETING TYPES

Once you have the right intent for your meeting, you have to pour it into the right container—the right *type* of meeting. When people invite you to "a meeting," it's a bit like asking you if you like "food." Yes, but which kind? The word "meeting" covers a huge range of different interactions. It is such a general term it has no real meaning any more. If you want successful meetings you have to be more specific. And that means understanding the fundamental reasons we humans meet—and always have.

Are you wearing fishnets to a tea party?

There's a scene in the comedy film *Bridget Jones's Diary* where the heroine turns up to a formal English country garden party in a Playboy Bunny costume. We learn that originally it was to be a "tarts and vicars" party but the theme was changed and Bridget has not received the message. This kind of mismatch is very funny to watch, but excruciating to experience.

And there's an important message here for meetings. Once you are clear about objective and underlying intent, it's important to choose the right *type* of meeting for the job in hand.

Let me start with a non-business example of what can happen if you don't: a parent-teacher meeting at my children's school.

The intent was clear enough. Parents and teachers were there to safeguard the education and wellbeing of the little people in their charge. So a checkmark for shared intent. And the objective was to talk about the curriculum for the coming year. The only problem was that the parents were envisaging one type of meeting and the teachers another type.

The meeting was billed as a "curriculum meeting." The teachers saw this as an *information sharing* meeting, a chance to communicate face to face what they had decided to teach during the year and how they intended to teach it. The parents, particularly the pushy ones, saw this as a *discussion* meeting, a chance to air their own views of what should be taught and how. One "side" saw the curriculum as a done deal, the other as a starting point. You can imagine how well the meeting went.

To use the Bridget Jones analogy, the teachers were in smart casual and the parents were in fishnets and fluffy bunny ears.

A meeting timed for 40 minutes ballooned as quite small points of information were hotly debated. The teachers, wrong-footed and running out of time, tried gallantly to manage things but ended up cutting off discussions mid-flow and even then had to bring the meeting to an end with the key points uncovered.

Pour the fuel of shared passion onto this smoldering mismatch of expectations and you turn a perfectly innnocent meeting into a really explosive situation.

If you want to avoid finding yourself wearing a "tarts and vicars" costume when everyone else is in evening wear to a fancy soirée, it's essential we talk about meeting types. Or, better still, archetypes.

Meet like a Caveman ...

My nutritionist says we should eat what a caveman would eat. It's an admirably simple idea. The human body evolved to ingest a diet of plant-derived carbohydrates with a bit of starch and the occasional meal of protein. It stands to reason that thousands of years on, a blip in evolutionary time, that's probably what we should still be eating. Instead we have massively complicated our diets and it is stressing us. We are an adaptable race, and our guts can accommodate the weirdness of the modern, highly processed, E-number-laced diet. We *can* adapt, but this takes its toll on our metabolism over time and ultimately it makes us ill. Nothing in our biology prepared us for Pot Noodle.

It made me ponder our meeting diet. When we mix up discussion, invention, and decision-making meetings, it's as if we are taking steak, a blueberry muffin, some pickles, one lobster, and a jar of peanut butter and blending them all together. The individual components are all delicious, but improperly combined they'd make an inedible gray sludge.

We're snacking, gorging, making ourselves sick. What if we simplified things and considered the archetypal reasons that humans meet? The world has changed a lot since we were strolling around on the prehistoric plains in bearskins— human nature very little.

I think we'd learn a lot about modern meetings (which we should have and which we should kick) when we travel back to the source and look for the ...

Seven Essential Reasons People Meet

I like to imagine they originate in our earliest history when two or more cavemen got together to ask the fundamental questions. I am translating here from the original "cave speak."

Imagine, if you will, it's two million years BC. Just before lunch. There's a commotion at the other end of the village and one of our fellow cave-dwellers is shouting, *"Did you see the mammoth?"* We gather around, eager for news, and the Meeting for Information is born. One of our group has data that is crucially important for our wellbeing, and a gathering is the best way to share that.

This brings us to the next question. *"Does anyone feel like mammoth for lunch?"* Everyone has an opinion about this. Some are vegetarians, others had mammoth last week. If social cohesion is to be preserved, everyone's voice needs to be heard in what becomes the archetypal Meeting for Discussion.

Mammoth seems a generally good idea. It's fresh, plump, and local. This is the age before supermarkets delivering your weekly grocery shopping, remember. When the talking is done, there's a third question to answer. *"Who will kill the mammoth?"* Time for the world's first Meeting for Decision. Options are collectively weighed and together you choose the one caveman who has just stepped out of the meeting to feed the pterodactyl (OK, I know I'm a few millennia out, but I like the imagery).

You have just thrust a spear into the hands of the hapless "volunteer" when you hear a monstrous trumpeting sound and another breathless caveman appears shouting, *"You know that mammoth you wanted to kill? It wants to kill us! What are we going to DO?"* Time for a Meeting for Problem-Solving. Homo sapiens's strong suit, this: the ability to conceptualize ways around problems. Best done in company, where we can pool our different points of view. It probably explains why mankind is still with us and the mammoth is not.

With the mammoth hunted and ready for cooking, the fifth great human question is heard: *"Does anyone have a new way to cook mammoth?"* We are a restlessly innovative species with a low boredom threshold. Mammoth stew is all very well, but what variations can we create on the basic theme? Time to hold a Meeting for Innovation and have everyone pool their ideas. With a bit of luck you come up with an answer that no one would have discovered individually—hence the logic of a meeting.

Dinner's done, your bellies are full and there's plenty of meat put away for winter. Then you notice there's still some mammoth fricassee left over. Time to visit the neighboring tribe and ask, *"Do you want to buy some mammoth?"* Like every Meeting for Selling through the ages that will follow this first one, there's a real power to physically meeting your customer so you can look them in the face as you seek to convince them to buy your product or idea.

The shadows lengthen, the crackling fire beckons, and with the day's work behind you, the last of the seven archetypal meeting questions arises—probably the most quintessentially human. *"Anyone want to come over to my cave and sing about the mammoth?"* It's the Meeting for Meeting, the social gathering or "get-together." It's a meeting whose main purpose is to meet; to form and strengthen relationships, social and personal bonds between members of the tribe.

MEETING 2,000,000 BC	THE SEVEN ARCHETYPAL MEETINGS
"Hey, everyone, I just saw a mammoth!"	Meet to Inform
"Who feels like mammoth for lunch?"	Meet to Discuss
"Who's going to kill the mammoth?"	Meet to Decide
"Er, angry mammoth. What now?"	Meet to (re)Solve
"Mammoth stew again???"	Meet to Innovate
"Wanna buy some mammoth?"	Meet to Sell
"Come over to my cave and talk mammoth?"	Meet to Meet

Let's look at those essential meetings in a little more detail, so you know how best to adapt and use them in your own organization.

The Meeting for Information

"Hey, everyone, I just saw a mammoth!"

Meetings for Information go by many names—reviews, presentations, updates, briefings, etc.

Their basic function is to share essential information. For much of human history physically gathering was the only effective way to do this collectively (rather than person by person). Medieval townspeople would gather at the well-head or in the market square to hear proclamations read and essential news called out. Today, in an age where information gushes at us in written, audio, and video form, it is no longer essential to meet to hear that the Hundred Years War has just broken out or that the Black Death will be paying a visit next Wednesday.

Now that we have the means to be instantly updated we can and should be very choosy about when we hold information meetings and why.

The Why of Information Meetings

"Information is not knowledge," said Einstein, reminding us that information *per se* is of little use. The word in*form*ation suggests "shaping," and I'd suggest that a very valuable use of such a meeting is to shape data (raw, objective fact) into meaning. Or, to put

169

it another way, a real information meeting creates *shared under-standing* in your organization.

In an age of information glut, these meetings will tend to proliferate. And the meeting can get overrun with peripheral detail. So it's essential we understand the intent of the meeting and include only that information which is relevant.

That said, do remember that many kinds of information are shared in a live meeting. The data is only one kind. When people meet to hear their leaders and colleagues share information, they are registering not only what is said, but the demeanor, tone, energy, and body language of those saying it. How you share information can massively affect how that information is inter-preted. "Our business is booming," says the CEO with the sweaty top lip, and analysts downgrade the company's AAA rating. "Times are tough, really tough," says the street-fighting entre-preneur with a glint in his eye, and the smart money flows in.

If you think the intent of your information meeting is simply *to inform*, think again. It's much more powerful to think you are sharing information:

> *to create confidence*
> *to give clear direction*
> *to surface dangers*
> *to become collectively smarter as a company*

The Who of Information Meetings

It's very difficult to un-invite people from a meeting they are used to attending. It's what I think of as "Uncle Vernon syndrome." Every family has one. He's boring, boorish, and smells faintly of weed-killer, but somehow you can't *not* invite Uncle Vernon to the wedding.

To help you make better choices about whom you should invite to an information meeting, ask yourself the following four questions:

> *Given the Intent, what is the key information (and I stress key) which we need to include? That means information that can't or shouldn't be shared in another way.*
> *Who absolutely needs to know this? And, of them, who needs to get the information first-hand, i.e. cannot be informed afterward by those attending?*
> *Why is this valuable (to you, to them, and to the business)?*
> *What would be lost if the meeting did not happen?*

Information Tourism

The same people who complain about having too many meetings are often to be found inviting themselves to information meetings because "they need to know what is going on." Information Tourism is rife in organizations these days, not least because the feeling endures that "knowledge is power." Be very clear in your own mind when inviting people to an information meeting that the people who attend genuinely need the information and don't just feel more important if they have it. Give them one of those VIP cards I recommended you to print earlier in the book and send them back where they came from.

The Where/When of Information Meetings

It is also important to consider whether this is an *input* or *output* meeting. Is the main information flowing into participants or being drawn out of them?

Input meetings are generally shorter and easier to stage. If you've spotted the mammoth and want your colleagues to know, you simply need them to gather round for long enough to get the information across and you are done. This kind of information meeting can be done standing up in a few minutes.

For an output meeting, where you are expecting participants to share information, it is good to create the feel of a forum; so set up the room "in the round" rather than formal rows. This will facilitate sharing.

Can we talk about PowerPoint for moment?

A critical question you have to ask yourself is "PowerPoint—yes or no?" And if "yes"—"how much?" PowerPoint is a classic example of a labor-saving technology which has made us work harder. It was originally developed (for Mac, surprisingly enough) as a substitute for those laborious slide projection presentations people used to slave over. It worked. And it didn't work. Slides are much, much easier to create now. Which is why there are MILLIONS of them clogging up our day.

Edward Tufte is a political science professor who has a sideline passion for information graphics and a blood feud with PowerPoint. Some of his key beefs, and they are hard to contest, are that this software program:

> *is used to guide and to reassure a presenter, rather than to enlighten the audience*
> *forces the audience to digest information in a linear sequence (whereas, with handouts, readers could browse and relate items at their leisure)*
> *is poorly designed, and*
> *encourages simplistic thinking*

Tufte went even further, indicting PowerPoint and its inept use within NASA for being a contributory factor in the catastrophic failure of the Space Shuttle Columbia. According to him, mission-critical engineering information was buried in eye-boggling, squinty little sub-sub-sub bullets at the bottom of slides when it should have been at the center of everyone's attention.

So if you are a slide-junky, be warned. PowerPoint can obscure the very points you want to get across. And overusing it can certainly lead to your colleagues wanting to murder you.

When I meet a client with the haunted look of a PowerPoint addict, here are three things I recommend:

1. *Use slides which support, but do not repeat, what you are saying*
2. *Use pictures where possible with the minimum of text (if any)*
3. *If you want to use PowerPoint as a memory aid for you, rather than a communication aid for your audience, then turn the projector around so the slides appear on the back wall. This way, you can see your cues and the audience can see you.*

You might also want to try a wonderfully simple technique for turning your PowerPoint presentations into real performances called "Pecha Kucha." Devised by a couple of PowerPoint-weary Tokyo-based architects Mark Dytham and Astrid Klein, Pecha Kucha (which is Japanese for "chatter") requires presenters to put their entire argument across in just 20 slides. Nothing too radical there, you may think. But the clever thing is that these slides are automatically timed to last 20 seconds each. If you are not done, the slide changes anyway. This makes for energized presentations where the audience admires panache as much as content. And it ensures that every presentation is done in 6 minutes 40 seconds—even if a windbag is speaking.

If you are looking for more fresh ways to share information, then read on.

The What of Information Meetings

Meetings for Information are usually much less engaging than they could be because of the routine way in which the information is shared. Common ways I see information shared include:

> *by rank (more senior players go first)*
> *by volume (the loudest wins)*
> *by chance (have an "organic" chat and hope the relevant information appears)*

Last time I checked, I had logged 27 ways of sharing information in a meeting. Here are my top ten. I am not necessarily proposing one over the other. What I do suggest is, if you are leading a Meeting for Information, you try a different method every time you meet. In this way, even a regular meeting can avoid feeling routine.

WAYS TO SHARE INFORMATION	EXAMPLE
By topic/issue	The leader asks participants to share any information they have about theme X ... If they have none, they stay quiet.
By urgency	Most urgent first and then by diminishing sense of urgency (as the participants see it). You can run this meeting as "urgent only," meaning only urgent topics are discussed. When you are done, or nothing's urgent, the meeting ends.
By importance	As above, except focusing on importance. It can be most helpful if the leader clearly stipulates criteria for what is and isn't important. Participants tend to think all their work is important.
What's essential	The leader provokes the participants to share only what *must* be shared this week/month. If it'll keep, don't take up meeting time.
Against the clock	Everyone has the same, predetermined time slot. Their challenge is to say what they need to in the time allowed. When the time is up they have to stop immediately, even mid-sentence. No exceptions.

By request	Participants are asked to share only information that they require help with (from other participants).
Show and Tell	Participants report what they have been up to since last meeting. It's a very good idea to time-limit.
Loose Ends	Participants share only what is not yet done since last time they met.
To Dos	Participants share only what they intend to do between now and the next meeting.
Any Questions	Participants share only information that requires further clarification (from other participants) before they can action it.

A friend of mine, the trainer and coach Richard Jacobs (www.yesindeed.com), has a really nice way of sharing information at the beginning of a team meeting. Richard says that the field of astronomy is one of the most necessarily collaborative in the world given that astronomers, wherever they may be, can only see "their" patch of night sky. To build a global picture, they have to share information. Richard will start a meeting by asking people to spend a couple of minutes telling their colleagues *what's in their patch of sky*. As a way of sharing information and creating connection between people, it works really well.

Things to watch out for:

A really useful information meeting elegantly shares information that it is ineffective, unwise, or downright life-threatening to share in another way (e.g. email, phone, etc). It is not:

A Reading Aid

Spoonfeeding colleagues too lazy or busy to have gotten around to the pre-reading.

Showing Your Homework

An opportunity to take people word by word through information they could have received elsewhere, with the intention of showing how well-informed you are.

A "Gab Fest"

Talking for its own sake. If you or your colleagues like to hear the sound of your own voices, get a Dictaphone. Most smartphones now come with one. Record yourself being clever and you can play it back when you have time in the car or the plane. But don't waste our time.

Recycling

Rehashing information that people already know. In the 1980s William Titus and Garold Stasser, two U.S. psychologists who were studying how groups communicated, discovered that most of what was discussed in the meetings they observed was already known. They were recycling the information not because they had environmental concerns but to firm up and get more support for their positions. Politicking rather than informing.

A Detail Deluge

A chance to submerge people in detail and dazzle with your mastery of the subject.

A Soapbox

There is a tendency to confuse "I want to share information" with "I am going to tell you what I think." Senior executives often have a blind spot in this area.

A Hack

This is a deft misuse of the information meeting which seriously destabilizes organizational culture. Here's how it works. The boss says: *Let's update each other so we all know what's going on.* What they really mean is: *I am going to pretend to share while actually getting you to tell me what you know, so I can look good to my boss.* This might work once, but as soon as people are wise to this approach, they become very reluctant to share high-quality information in future.

The Meeting for Discussion

"Who feels like mammoth for lunch?"

Juror 8: I just want to talk.

Juror 7: Well, what's there to talk about? Eleven men in here think he's guilty. No one had to think about it twice except you ...

Juror 8: I'm not trying to change your mind. It's just that ... we're talking about somebody's life here. We can't decide it in five minutes. Supposing we're wrong?

Juror 7: Supposing we're wrong? Supposing this whole building should fall down on my head? You can suppose anything!

Juror 8: That's right.

Twelve Angry Men **(MGM, 1957)**

The Why of Discussion Meetings

In the tense courtroom drama classic, *Twelve Angry Men*, Juror 8, played by Henry Fonda says he *"just wants to talk,"* but what he really wants is a discussion.

The word comes from the Latin *discutio*, meaning *to shake apart*. And that's precisely what our Henry manages to do, shaking the jury's initial verdict apart, challenging prejudice, forcing fellow jurors to re-examine their knee-jerk reactions until, two hours of tense drama later, the 11-to-one *guilty* becomes a unanimous *not guilty*. That's a great justification for discussion.

The same happens in our house. OK, we don't lock ourselves away, curse, and throw furniture at the camera method-acting style, but discovering where the Pearl family wants to spend Saturday afternoons, or which costume drama DVD we are going to watch entails serious discussion between my wife, children, and me.

Discussion is a mechanism humans came up with so we could find out what we really think about things.

As Henry points out, we "can suppose anything." Our minds are full of supposings, assumptions, and stale thinking. Very often what we *think* is actually what we previously *thought*. And discusssion updates it.

It's been said that many of us *talk to think*. We don't know what we really think until we hear ourselves say it. And others *think to talk*. That is, we need to hear what others say and digest this so we can formulate our own perspective.

The Who of Discussion Meetings

A real discussion clearly requires a good blend of different perspectives. You want to pick people who can look at a topic in a way that will challenge the blind spots, prejudices, and supposings.

When you get together it's worth reminding each other that real discussions are not:

> *saying what you think others want to hear*
> *holding back what you really think till after the meeting*
> *the same as argument*
> *endless*
> *a perfunctory rubber-stamping of ideas you know the boss has already decided upon*

The Where of Discussion Meetings

Tony Blair upset centuries of tradition—and legions of civil servants—when he moved the locus of his governmental discussion from the formality of the Cabinet Room to his own office, "The Den" as it became known. The "Sofa Cabinet" wasn't to everyone's taste, nor was Mr. Blair, but it does serve to remind us that a stuffy, starchy boardroom may not be the most conducive atmosphere for a real discussion.

Think about the different places in your business where you could be holding discussions, including the less formal.

I remember walking into the boardroom at the Dutch apparel company Mexx for a discussion about their brand. The room is a super-cool, minimalist glass box that is cantilevered out of one side of their offices so it hangs over space. Very groovy, but nothing to do with the socially-aware, grassroots origins of the company that we were meeting to discuss. I asked my client Ashish Sensarma to take us around the building and show us the real Mexx. We were in and out of design studios, wardrobes, showrooms, cafeterias, a smoking room—and finally, in the garage, we found a school bus fixed up into a mobile store. Very funky. Very popular. Very Mexx. And that is where we had the meeting.

Instead of boardroom table, perhaps think dining table. Food is a great stimulus to discussion. For our mammoth-eating ancestors, eating was a moment of vulnerability when you couldn't defend yourself. Inviting another caveperson to join you at a meal was therefore a symbol of trust. Today, there is still something about sharing food around a table that helps us drop our defences and really discuss things.

Discussions can—and I venture to say should—get noisy. *Discussion* is, after all, related to *percussion*. So hold it somewhere you won't disturb others. And where participants will feel comfortable to be boisterous if they want.

The What of Discussion Meetings

Real discussion, especially in a conference call, needs to be led, with someone paying close attention to what's happening. In these busy, busy days it is easy to skate over the surface of important topics. It takes meeting leadership to ensure a discussion is allowed the time it needs and also to conclude it when the time comes.

Three ways you know when the discussion is complete—or needs to be paused for a refresh:

> *The subject has been thoroughly explored from (at least) as many viewpoints as there are participants.*
> *It runs out of energy.*
> *It turns into something else—a showcase of opinions, a battle, a gossip.*

The content of your discussion is clearly a function of the discussion's Intent. What is this discussion *for*? For example, it could be:

> **a Discussion for Clarity** (*e.g. does this mean what we think it means?*)
> **a Discussion for Assurance** (*have we covered all the bases?*)
> **a Discussion for Understanding** (*let's collectively analyze the problem so we can collectively tackle it).*

Things to watch out for

One or more participants dominating the discussion. The meeting leader needs to challenge windbags. One good way to do this is to use a device my kids developed for when I "go on" too long about the merits of piano practice etc, etc, etc. They give me the "thumbs up" sign, which means in our agreed code, "I heard what you said, Dad, and repeating it in different ways doesn't mean I am going to hear it more." It's what we call the "Got It, Move On" rule, and I have found it works really well in the workplace. Certainly, far better than the gesture where you move your hand across your throat to signify you are about to cut your own throat, or the speaker's.

Another elegant way to tackle this is to use the rule described by Peter Miller in his engaging book *Smart Swarm* about collective intelligence. He cites the tale of Vermont, where budgets are still set by the townspeople themselves in genuine Town Hall meetings. To contain those participants who love the sound of their own voices, the meeting conveners follow a ground rule proposed by the Victorian soldier-turned-meeting-designer Brigadier General Henry Martyn Robert. This soldier-turned-meeting engineer compiled a list of meeting dos and don'ts ("Robert's Rules of Order") which hold good in Vermont to this day. The rule, which is beautifully simple in its ability to curb the long-winded, goes: "Nobody speaks twice till everybody has spoken once."

You can see how well this would work in your own meetings, particularly if you agree that one of your colleagues holds back till the end of the meeting, thus effectively silencing any potential meeting hijacker!

Another phenomenon you need to be aware of in discussion meetings is Stacking. This is where various different topics go into a circling pattern—like planes being "stacked" for landing at a busy airport. They go around and around, neither arriving nor leaving. Like a good air traffic controller, if you see this you need to either land the topic ("I think we are clear on that point now, let's move on") or send it to another destination ("We don't have time to do that justice now—we'll discuss in our meeting on ...").

Why not try a Debate?

Debate is the first cousin of Discussion. It can act as the middle step between Discussion and Decision.

Debate is a highly structured discussion that is designed to see whether the participants are *for* or *against* a particular idea by pitting it against its opposite. In a debate the gloves can really come off as one "side" pummels the other's idea as hard as it can.

Properly done, it's a wonderful exercise and helps teams really feel they are making fully tested decisions.

Debate is a very helpful way of breaking a deadlock in a discussion. It also, I find, has the very helpful side-effect of separating people from their dearly held opinions; particularly when you ask a team that is ferociously arguing "for" a particular course of action, to switch sides and start championing the complete opposite. This technique, which I understand is practiced in various schools of Bhuddism, not only keeps us intellectually nimble but reminds us that we are supposed to have opinions; they are not supposed to have us.

The important thing is to know when the time for talk is done. As one-time British Prime Minister Clement Atlee put it: *Democracy means government by discussion, but it is only effective if you can stop people talking.*

Discussion is supposed to lead to decision. Which is where are heading now.

The Meeting for Decision

"Who's going to kill the mammoth?"

There is a reason the word *decide* comes from the Latin *decidere*, meaning *"to cut off."* It represents an end of the discussion. It's the rap of the judge's gavel or the auctioneer's hammer that signifies the law has spoken, the last bids are in. Or it should be.

Very often decision meetings in business don't conclude with a clear decision. And when they do, those decisions are often contested afterwards, overturned and/or rediscussed at the next meeting.

"Our meetings are indecisive" is one of the leading complaints I hear from clients. And I suggest this is because they are not setting up their meetings as Meetings for Decision.

The Why of Decision Meetings

The underlying intent of decision meetings—of decision making in general—is to move from thought and talk to action.

Decisions are the motive force that propels us forward. The opposite is paralysis. I have seen clients labor for months to achieve a 100 percent correct decision, only to see the conditions change and undermine the beautifully crafted decision they were hoping to make. In these days of warp speed change, 80 percent right often has to be good enough, especially when you get to the do-or-die point where a decision must be made. As Teddy Roosevelt once said, *"In any moment of decision the best thing you can do is the right thing, the next best thing is the wrong thing, and the worst thing you can do is nothing."*

The Who of Decision Meetings

Whom do you invite to decision meetings? Well, decision makers would be helpful. How often do you find that the key person with the capacity to make a decision is not actually in the meeting? If this happens, I'd advise you to stop the meeting and get on with your day.

Also, if you have set up the decision meeting right (see below), then the number of people who need to be at a decision meeting can be very small. The number of people who *want* to be at decision meetings can be very large. There was probably considerable prestige for our mammoth-hunting ancestors to be "in at the kill." This is the modern equivalent. There is both kudos and status that your colleagues may associate with being present when decisions are made. Even if it's only to nod and say sagely, "I agree with Nick."

If you want to restrict the number of people present at a decision meeting to those who have a material role to play, I suggest you insure those who are not invited are kept well informed about any decisions directly relevant to them.

The How (and What) of Decision Meetings

If you are having problems with decision meetings and want to improve them, take a look at what is happening before the meeting and after it. The problem is rarely the meeting itself; but the process leading up to and following it.

Good decisions, particularly important ones, take adequate preparation. For every hour Ron, the top-flight Management Consultant, spends in a decision meeting, he spends three in bilateral and ad hoc meetings to prepare for that decision.

He makes sure everyone has the relevant information, that all reasonable questions are answered in advance, and has checked in with each of the attendees to know what is going on "below the waterline" in their attitude to the decision.

Other essential pre-work includes:

> *approaching outside experts to see what they think*—collecting all relevant contributions from colleagues
> *listening to customers*
> *checking you have the money and resources to implement the decision if you make it*
> *making sure that this is the right time to be making the decision. As one Chief Legal Officer put it to me, is the issue* decision ripe? *If not, then bear in mind what the pithy 17th-century author and soldier Lord Falkland said.* "When it is not necessary to make a decision, it is necessary not to make a decision." *And he wrote a book called* A Treatise on Infallibility, *so he should know!*

Now add a Deadline

Decisions by definition happen when the time for talking runs out. If there isn't a deadline this may never happen. So create one, even if it's artificial. Crisis has its origin in the Greek word *krinein* meaning "decide." They work well as a pair.

Yes, you may have to act before you are 100 percent sure, as we have already mentioned. But if a decision is essential, that's better than no decision.

As another president, Franklin D. Roosevelt, told his Head of Labor in a particularly difficult moment,"One thing is sure. We have to do something. We have to do the best we know how at the moment. If it doesn't turn out right, we can modify it as we go along."

If, when it came to the crunch, eight out of ten was sufficient for not one Leader of the Free World, but two, I guess it should be adequate for us.

If you've done your pre-work well, you have a fighting chance that the assembled decision makers will either have a proposal to green-light or a very focused range of tested options to choose from.

But your work doesn't end there.

Enroling people in the decision

It's just possible that there are people who don't agree with the decision that has been made. And here lie the seeds of the decision spiral where what has been decided gets undercut outside the room and then revisited and re-discussed at some point in the future. In the wake of a decision meeting you may well have to be enroling the participants to treat "the" decision as "their" decision. They may not be able to agree, but they are required to accept. It was, I think, Lord Tebbit who, when asked for his reactions on being routed by Labour in the 1997 U.K. elections, said, "Democracy means—sometimes you lose." He may not have liked the electorate's decision, but it was one he was clearly going to have to accept and live with.

Promoting the decision

When Second Lieutenant Hiroo Onoda was found on the Phillipine Island of Lubang still fighting the Second World War in 1974, it was because no one had adequately communicated to him that Japan had decided to surrender 29 years earlier. I can imagine he was ticked off. And you probably feel the same when you learn about an important decision too late.

The Japanese army did drop leaflets in 1945 and again in the fifties, but Lt. Onda didn't read the first and didn't believe the second. Had email been invented, the notification would no doubt have gone into his Junk folder. It's a salutary reminder to communicate important decisions promptly and effectively. And to check that the communication has been received.

When this doesn't happen, you are likely to see decisions endlessly re-discussed because people simply don't know what has been decided. Restricting access to decision meetings may make a lot of sense for the productivity of your company. But do tell people what went on behind closed doors. And not in an email. If it is a major decision, the meeting may need to be followed—not just preceded—by bilateral meetings, so people understand what has been decided and appreciate what this means for them.

Tracking the decision

Tracking completes the post-decision hat-trick. Quite simply, have you checked that what you decided has been done? When this doesn't happen it's like leaving the third leg off a stool. And the whole process falls over, with you on top of it.

A great way to start the meeting following any decision meeting is to ask the question:

> *"Has what we decided been put into action? And if not, why not?"*

It's also crucial to look back at decisions you have made in the past and ask:

> *"Was that decision a good one?"*

As the wise Peter Drucker puts it: "Checking the results of a decision against its expectations shows executives what their strengths are, where they need to improve, and where they lack knowledge or information."

I advise clients to put a slot into their meetings called "this time last year," when they look back 52 weeks to see how brilliant or fallible their decisions proved. It can be very instructive!

The Meeting for Invention

"Mammoth stew again???"

Human beings invent stuff. Arrowheads, steam engines, internets, odor-eating inner soles.

It is thought that the reason Modern Man supplanted Neanderthals as the dominant human species is that, while Neanderthals were physically better equipped to handle the challenges of life on the planet (stronger, tougher), our ancestors were smarter. When Neanderthals had eaten their fill of mammoth, they would probably roll over for a snooze. Meanwhile our predecessors were skinning and boning the unfortunate creature to produce raw materials for clothing, shelter, and home furnishings. Their ability to *come up with something new* is the main reason we are here. Invention is what we do. We can this do by ourselves—the solitary artist laboring to produce a masterpiece in an attic is an enduring (if slightly Hollywood-esque) icon of modern civilization. But creativity is more often a collective affair. Great painters had their muses, great playwrights have actors to try ideas out on, and I like to think that great novelists probably hop into bed and bore their partners with the day's scribblings. Would we even have heard of Archimedes if Mrs. A hadn't run him that bath? We'll never know. Hence, the Meeting for Invention.

The Why of Invention Meetings

A real invention meeting is a collective gathering that produces ideas which none of the participants would have had individually.

I suggest that in a good meeting for invention, you don't have the ideas, they have you.

As I mentioned earlier, when I am not working in business, I work on stage as an improviser. The company, Impropera, makes up operas on the spot. None of us knows the storyline, words, or music in advance, it is all created spontaneously when one performer offers an idea and the others accept and build on that idea. The net result is one that we have all participated in, but for which none of us can take individual credit. The feeling I have at the end of a successful improvised show is not *I sang well* but *we were sung well*.

Clearly business meetings are different—no one gets stabbed in the heart with a cooking spatula for one thing—but a really successful invention meeting will often feel similar. A great new idea grows from a seed that is built on by others. Bit by bit this escalates from a glimmer into a potentially do-able innovation. Pixar, no slouch at inventiveness as a business, are clear about the power of collective inventiveness. As Andrew Stanton, director of the multi-million-dollar hit *Finding Nemo*, puts it:

> The thing that finally makes it on the screen is all about rewrite, rewrite, rewrite. A good portion of the rewrite process is not done by the screenwriter at a word processor, it's the story department. It's the guys who sit in a room with

*you for close to two years batting out ideas, countering your
ideas, drawing up story panels, putting them up on the wall,
pitching things, putting things on a reel down in Editorial.
It's a very malleable, messy, glorious process.*

If collective inventiveness has gone well, no individual can take
credit—though watch everyone try if the idea is a good 'un. In
fact, our individual minds are usually playing catch-up, trying to
figure out what happened. And that's the point, I think. If the
invention meeting is set up right, it is a mechanism to *go faster
than your mind normally allows you.*

The Who of Invention Meetings

Invention meetings don't have an upper limit on size. I have run
mass brainstorms—I call them Idea Blizzards—for upwards of
1500 people. Equally, a few people sitting around a table and the
back of an envelope can be just as effective. And there's a little
less mess to clear up afterwards.

It kind of depends on how much creativity you want to release
and how much time you are prepared to invest, sifting through
possibilities and tidying up the mess afterwards.

Do be sure that you include people who describe themselves
as "uncreative." They will probably come up with the best ideas
of all.

The Where of Invention Meetings

The key words I'd suggest here are *Disrupt* and *Stimulate*.

THE SEVEN BASIC MEETING TYPES

Disruption

Humans—and the organizations they create—are prone to become routine if you let them. Invention and Routine don't go well together. As creativity guru Kevin Kelly puts it forcefully, "Equilibrium is Death!" For this reason, it's helpful if you stage the invention meeting in a way that breaks the pattern.

A full-blown retreat to Barbados is not necessary. But a change of scenery, even a change of rooms, might be helpful. Comfortable chairs instead of formal ones. Get rid of the boardroom table and reduce distance between people. Get some music, some fresh air, some pizza.

Stimulation

The imagination runs on stimulus. If you want a successful invention meeting, fill up the tank first. For some companies "stimulus" seems to equal colored pens and a beanbag. It's a start, but stimulus comes in many forms. Here are a few examples that I have seen work well:

> *Make an urgent request. The classic example is 3M reminding employees that their revenue three years hence would depend on products they had not yet invented. One company I work with has predicted that, if they don't start getting inventive, their profit margin will dwindle from high 8 figures to virtually nothing in the next five years. I think that qualifies as an urgent request.*
> *Bring in a pile of magazines you would never normally read (the more unusual the better).*

> *Have a stack of unrelated art photographs you can sift through to tweak the non-verbal areas of the brain to life. We sometimes hold invention meetings in art galleries for this reason.*
> *Share film or YouTube clips that could be relevant (and fun).*
> *Watch what your customers are watching, eat what they are eating, wear what they are wearing.*
> *Awaken all the senses. That means food, sound, music, light. It is said that when Leonardo painted the* Mona Lisa *he hired musicians and jugglers to keep his mood creative. You don't need to go to those lengths, but some adjustments in the environment are going to pay dividends.*

The philosopher and management writer Charles Handy (*The Empty Raincoat: The Age of Unreason*) offered me a wonderful example of how disruption and simulation can create the ideal conditions for inventiveness.

St. George's House, hidden away in the grounds of Windsor Castle, was founded as a place where people of "influence and responsibility" could discreetly meet and discuss the issues of the day. Charles, who was its Warden from 1977 to 1981, describes a torrid meeting which was changed by a shift of place and mood.

> *The Bishop of Coventry wanted to convene a meeting about the future of work in Coventry. Windsor Castle was a sufficiently seductive venue for those taking part. The group was very diverse—teachers, businesspeople, politicians, trade unionists. In fact, it was so diverse that the meeting*

quickly became a cycle of recrimination, with the various factions blaming each other.

We were not getting very far, so we paused the meeting and suggested people go into the chapel for Choral Eucharist. It wasn't intended to be a religious moment, just to change the atmosphere. I don't know what happened— something about the Mozart Mass, I expect—but when they returned to the meeting the mood had completely changed. Everyone started making offers to each other. The education people started saying they'd help keep an eye on young people even after they leave school, the man from Jaguar said he'd offer apprenticeships to 14-year-olds. And so on.

We'd moved from being a committee to a team. Committees are a bargaining process, where everyone's after something and they all end up trading. Teams tend to have a shared purpose and common cause. If you want to get really inventive, you have to turn a committee into a team.

The What of Invention Meetings

A good invention meeting will have two phases.

The first phase, call it *divergent*, is all about letting the ideas flow, the more the merrier, with no pressure or requirement to assess how good they are. I think of this phase as turning on the faucet in a house that has been unoccupied for a while. You have to let the stagnant water flow for a while before the clear, fresh supply starts to gush out. So give this first phase adequate time. The first "new" ideas that emerge will often be old thinking. It takes time and energy to get genuinely new thoughts into the room.

The second, *convergent* phase is where you begin to filter, sort, and assess the ideas. I say begin, because you might want to set up a separate meeting to do this.

Watch out!

The great enemy of true invention is Judgement, particularly premature. If it appears too early in the process it will stifle the flow of divergent ideas. It will say things like "this won't work" or "this is a dumb idea" or "how would you implement this?" There will be a time for your new idea to face rigorous questioning, but the first invention meeting definitely isn't it. Countless innovations seemed crazy initially ("This internet thing will never catch on," said leading scientist Clifford Stoll in 1995). That's their job.

I know clients who are desperate to be more inventive, but who back off from full-blown invention meetings. Instead they relegate invention, the lifeblood of their future revenue, to a peremptory "brainstorm" at the yearly management retreat. Clearly there is a balance to be struck here. As the highly successful Design Consultancy IDEO puts it: "Nobody wants to run an organization on feeling, intuition, and inspiration, but an over-reliance on the rational and the analytical can be just as risky." Or as an über consultant I know once confided to me, "It is our job to kill off crazy ideas for our clients. My concern is we are not having enough crazy ideas to kill off."

So make sure that invention meeting happens, and happens frequently.

The Meeting for (Re)Solution

"Er, angry mammoth. What now?"

"The problem is not that there are problems. The problem is expecting otherwise and thinking that having problems is a problem."

This nicely circular statement comes from the popular American psychiatrist Theodore Rubin, neatly reminding us that one of the endearing characteristics of humanity is our ability to create problems for ourselves. As a race, we just don't do the problem-free thing. Stasis scares us. Equilibrium gives us the heeby-jeebies. It may be peaceful but it's boring.

They say every new stage of evolution brings its own patholo-gies with it. Certainly, the minute we achieve a bit of harmony, someone or something comes along to upset it.

There's a myth that lurks in the back of our mind which suggests there is something we can do to make the problems go away for good. Advertisers capitalize on this to sell us everything from life insurance to liposuction. Buy this and you'll be free from cares, woes, and cellulite. Drug cartels are another sector that trade on our hankering for a cloudlessly problem-free "high."

The psychiatrist and holocaust survivor Viktor Frankl, a man who had known his fair share of problems, puts it beautifully when he says in his inspiring book *Man's Search for Meaning*: "What man actually needs is not a tensionless state but rather the striving and struggling for some goal worthy of him. What he needs is not the discharge of tension at any cost, but the call of a potential meaning waiting to be fulfilled by him."

The fact is, the tidal cycle of creating and curing problems is an integral part of life—business life, in particular. So are Meetings for (re)Solving.

The Why of (re)Resolution Meetings

We learn from solving the problems we've created. And then we create new problems to learn from. When you see problem-solving as part of a learning cycle, you transform the (re)solution meeting from a chore to an essential, energizing aspect of your business.

Whether you're tackling a chronic, long-term issue or managing an immediate crisis, it's powerful to think that the problem is there to teach you something. The purpose of the meeting is to tune through the static and find an answer that is there—but which you haven't seen yet.

And because we no longer have mammoths to kill to prove our worth to the tribe, we like to create mammoth-sized problems. Ones that we have to meet together to solve.

The Who of (re)Solution Meetings

It's helpful to think of the people who attend a problem-solving meeting as a series of components you are assembling into a mechanism which is far smarter and quicker than any of the individuals involved. Don't let the Frankensteinian power go to your head, but you are building a "group mind" that's more effective than a single one.

The complexity of the problems we can now create mean it's a time for intelligent networks and using the wisdom of crowds. Let's unleash the spirit of the beehive. As the book by Barry Libert and John Spector puts it succinctly, *we* are smarter than *me*.

One of the keys to a great problem-solving meeting is to invite one representative from every function or department that is affected by the problem. Each of them will have a different view of the problem and, just as importantly, a stake in solving it.

We all have our perspective, our own angle on a situation. By definition this means we don't see what's beyond the limits of that point of view. We all have our blind spots. The more expert we are, the more certain we are that what we see is all there is. Multi-functional problem solving can annoy us because it shows us the limits of our thinking. But it's really helpful if you want to build up a detailed picture of what's really happening, not just what you individually are convinced is happening.

Once you have the right, multi-perspective problem-solving team assembled, take a leaf out of the old Hollywood producer's book. Lock them in a room, give them a tight deadline, and order a lot of pizza.

The How of (re)Solution Meetings

Joking aside, choosing the location of a (re)solution meeting can take a bit of emotional intelligence on the part of the meeting organizer.

This is particularly important where what you are resolving is a conflict between people or parties. There is a reason why the U.S. Government maintains a rural, dress-down, feel-at-home facility like Camp David deep in Maryland's Catocin Mountains to hash out those explosive geo-political issues. A non-professional milieu can help people put aside their professional armor and just connect as people.

Also, getting away from the routines of everyday life is a way of elevating our minds above everyday thinking. As Einstein put it, "The significant problems we face cannot be solved at the same level of thinking we were at when we created them."

The What of (re)Solution Meetings

We don't really have space to do justice to this knotty subject here, but I'd like to suggest that the effectiveness of your problem-solving meeting is directly related to the quality of the *questions* you ask in the meeting. Here are some questions which I have found really work well in accelerating meetings to creative solutions.

What do we have to assume for this to be true?
Before you examine the problem, examine your assumptions about the problem. If the assumptions are false, very often the problem shifts dramatically or even disappears.

What happens if we do nothing?
It's worth asking this just to check the problem is worth spending your collective time on. If it isn't, then don't.

What would we do, if we could not fail?
It's a question beloved of the pony-tail-toting motivational speaker but it's useful here. Our problem-solving (like our inventiveness) is often constrained by our fear of getting things wrong. We may back away from a daring solution because it looks too risky. Try running a 45-minute session in which people fess up to things they would try if they couldn't fail. Filter out the lunatic ones, by all means. But hang on to anything that has a grain of possibility in it.

If we imagine a future where this is solved, what do we have to do to get there?
If you can't see your way around a problem, try this natty NLP technique. Instead of figuring out how you get from *here* to *there*, imagine a future where you have solved the problem and then work your way back! Logically, this shouldn't work, but it does. That's because you are using imagination not logic.

Is this problem, that we are trying to solve, the right problem?
A pretty crucial question, this. In the film *Apollo 13* everyone is rushing around working out the correct angle, fuel burn, and speed for the stricken module to land when a quiet-spoken electrical engineer points out that the electrical power will peter out long before re-entry is even relevant. A team of PhDs have been

diligently "working the problem" as requested. It was just the wrong problem.

As Marvin Bauer, the doyen of world-leading problem-solvers McKinsey and Company, liked to remind his colleagues, *"Make sure you are answering the right question, not just fixing a signal of the problem."*

How are we, the problem-solvers, contributing to this problem? Sometimes problem-solving lacks real energy because you have the feeling that the solution is beyond your control or influence. Our capacities are dulled by the sense that "we can't do anything about this." I always find it's uncomfortable but ultimately empowering to be forced to recognize that we are all, in some way, contributing to the problem we are seeking to solve.

If this problem had no solution, what could we learn anyway? My dad likes to say (loosely quoting the waggish pundit Bernard Levin), "If the question you are considering has a simple answer, it's almost certainly not worth discussing." The unanswerable question is still worth asking. The business world tends to think the absolute opposite: all problems have a solution and are there to be solved.

Great artists are perfectly happy to ponder the unfathomable. When Shakespeare asks *"To be or not to be?"* he is not expecting a black-and-white answer. The average business type would want to end *Hamlet* with some metrics and market research to prove that Being is statistically preferable to Not Being, though Not Being is more cost-effective year on year.

Because some problems don't have solutions, it doesn't mean they aren't worth puzzling at. Indeed, trying to answer the unanswerable is very good for getting us to think in new ways. The conversation can have very useful spin-offs for an organization.

Dilemma time

If you want to sharpen your team, toss them an occasional dilemma; that's a question where there is no right or wrong answer. Dilemmas force us to choose between two (or more) rights or two (or more) wrongs. They force us to think deeper, to engage our judgement, experience, and values, not just our intellects.

Is this an either/or problem?

Our binary minds often fall into the either/or thinking. I remember facilitating a meeting in Mallorca for the financial services company Skandia where a strategy conversation had become deadlocked. One group was arguing for plan A and the other for plan B. They turned to Nick Poytnz-Wright, their low-key but fiercely intelligent CEO, for a decision: A or B? Nick, who had been carefully watching the problem-solving process as it spiraled, said, "I don't think the answer is A *or* B. I think the answer is A *then* B." In other words, both options were right, they just needed to be implemented in sequence.

Are we actually disagreeing?

This is a very salutary question to ask when there is a conflict in a team. Or there appears to be. I have seen teams that fundamentally agree about how a problem should be solved, arguing with each other about nuances. It's what I call "furious agreement" and can exhaust a group's energy far more than an out-and-out impasse. Very often there is ego involved, with people bidding for things to be done "their way" and thereby to gain prestige. Jenny, a wise and extremely able senior civil servant once shared her golden rule: "You can get anything done in this world provided you don't want to get credit." If resolution is deadlocked because of an argument about means, see if you can direct people to the outcome—and get them to see that it doesn't matter how we get there. As long as we get there. In other words, remind them they actually are in agreement.

This is also a time-honored technique of conflict resolution: find common ground and work your way back from there.

The Meeting for Selling

"Wanna buy some mammoth?"

According to the Bible, the whole human experience began with a sales pitch ...

> And the woman said to the serpent, "We may eat of the fruit of the trees of the garden; but God said, 'You shall not eat of the fruit of the tree which is in the midst of the garden, neither shall you touch it, lest you die.'" But the serpent said to the woman, "You will not die."
> **Genesis 3**

That serpent is a "closer." Eve knows she shouldn't eat. A moment on the lips, an eon on the hips. But that serpent knows his customer and, with a gentle nudge, the sale is made. Not only that, but Eve then acts like a franchisee or customer-advocate and immediately sells the naughty-but-nice apple to Adam ...

> *So when the woman saw that the tree was good for food, and that it was a delight to the eyes, and that the tree was to be desired to make one wise, she took of its fruit and ate; and she also gave some to her husband, and he ate. Then the eyes*

of both were opened, and they knew that they were naked;
and they sewed fig leaves together and made themselves
aprons.

We just witnessed the birth of Marriage, Sin and, it would seem, the Clothing Industry. And all through a sale.

The Why of Selling Meetings

Selling is quintessentially human. The minute we had more than we needed, we started gathering to swap, trade, and sell the surplus.

Selling is not just what the Sales department does. We are all selling, all the time. This includes selling stories, ideas, products, and, let's not forget, ourselves.

We'll even sell when there's no intrinsic value in the sale. One month on a desert island and we'll be trading shells for campfire lighting services and offering each other cut-price coconuts "on special." There's something about the dynamic of exchange that we humans enjoy.

Often clients aren't aware that they are holding a "selling" meeting. They think they are *presenting* or *communicating* or *training* and overlook the active "selling" that is required to get their ideas "bought" by their audience. The result is underpowered, rather dull meetings. Like a movie with the sound turned down. And the brightness.

In the performing arts we talk about "selling" a song. It is a reminder we are in a relationship with our customer, the audience. The job of the performer is to bring the material alive, to put our energy and ourselves into what we are communicating. If we don't make the "sale," we don't eat.

A good recommendation, then, when you are setting the intent of your meeting is to consider: do I need to *sell* the idea/concept/ plan to my colleagues/customers? And if so, prepare to perform.

The Who of Selling Meetings

Where does a good salesperson have their attention 99 percent of the time? On their customers. They focus on what the customer is thinking, feeling, wanting. They adjust their "patter" accordingly. In a selling meeting, more than any other, it's not what you say that's important, it is what the audience hears. So do your research. Whether the meeting is external (e.g. a pitch for new business) or internal (e.g. selling a new idea to your colleagues), find out:

> *When did they last buy something like this?*
> *Who else is selling comparable things to them and/or competing for their attention?*
> *What's their budget?*
> *What turns them on/off (tastes, preferences, hot buttons)?*
> *What is their unexpressed need?*

And, last but not least,

> *Are they in the market for what you are selling?*

Even polished operators can slip up on this last one. Ron, the Management Consultant, confided to me that he had recently been at a very high-stakes pitch meeting where, 53 minutes into the scheduled hour, the CEO said, "Nothing you are offering me is remotely useful to my problem. Goodbye." Or words to that effect. Ron suspects that the actual problem was a business crisis which was diverting the CEO's attention. But if that's true, it's also a vital piece of pre-meeting intel. Don't hold a sales meeting when the customer doesn't have the mind space for it. *Are you listening, you folk who phone me up from India on a Saturday evening trying to sell me insurance? Do you hear me, Brenda and James from Mysore???*

The How of Selling Meetings

As someone who has grown up in "showbiz," my own recommendation to you would be to think of any selling meeting as a performance. That doesn't mean being artificial or actorish. It means treating the customer as your audience and the meeting as your stage.

All the performer's golden rules apply:

> *Know your lines*
> *Make sure the audience can see and hear you*
> *Don't bump into the furniture*

One thing all performers like to do is to check the venue in advance and make sure the room or hall is working for them. If there is technology, make sure it is functioning well. The simple rule is: if it can go wrong, it will go wrong.

The other thing to remember about presentation technology (PowerPoint, film, audio) is this. The audience is just as interested in the seller as in what they are selling. It's tempting to hide behind the tricks and the techno, but being sold to still boils down to looking someone in the eye and thinking, "Do I believe you?" One reason the late lamented Steve Jobs's epic product launches were so successful is that, amid all the digital paraphernalia, his own passion for the product poured out.

If you are planning to use technical aids, do yourself a favor and rehearse without any, "unplugged" as it were, to check that what you are selling is compelling even without the bells and whistles. If your case is limp *without* those fancy color slides, it will still be limp *with* them. Shots of Magic Johnson in mid slam-dunk or an Hawaiian sunset do not a compelling story make. And the audience knows it.

Rehearsal, by the way, is an essential part of performance. And should be integral to any important Meeting for Selling you are doing. Sportspeople train, performers practice, brain surgeons try things once or twice before they wield the knife; it's only in business where we fling ourselves into high-stakes situations trusting in our ability to "wing it."

Rehearsal means knowing the flow of your story, distributing parts to people with specialist knowledge (as appropriate), anticipating the possible objections/problems the customer may have and preparing plausible responses. Rehearsal is not a "drill," repeating a procedure so it runs smoothly almost without you needing to think about it. Burning buildings, busted race car tires and failing airplanes all call for drills. But going into a meeting over-drilled makes you inflexible when the unexpected happens. Which it always does. Rehearsal isn't about getting it *right*, it's about giving you *options*. If you have rehearsed the 20 pages you have prepared you can put them aside in the meeting and "just be yourself." The apparent spontaneity of the "natural" salesperson is usually a carefully cultivated illusion that takes significant preparation.

The What of Selling Meetings

A buddy of mine, the web marketing expert J.C. Mac, claims all you need for a successful sale is "a short rap, a small box and a loud trumpet." The box is to stand on so you can be seen in the crowd; the trumpet is to get your audience's attention; the short rap is a compelling story they can understand and remember. Ask yourself this, before you next go into a meeting for selling: what's the simplest way you can have your message heard, understood, and remembered? And here are two more questions you may find useful:

What are you really selling?
I ask because I think we often lose the big picture on this one. We get fascinated by the features when we should be focusing on the benefits.

I often see business leaders fretting the night before launching a new strategy or vision. They are worrying needlessly about whether the logic is watertight, the numbers are accurate and the *Rocky* soundtrack is going to come in at the right moment. What they need to remember is that the audience isn't buying logic, numbers, or tacky emotional cues. They simply want to believe in their CEO. Is she plausible, sympathetic, clear? Rather than worry over content details, she'd be better off getting a good night's sleep so she's relaxed and naturally engaging the following day.

Are they buying what you are selling?

A much-quoted story was told to me by the one-time chairman of J. Walter Thompson, Jeremy Bullmore. He'd been called in by Black & Decker to help them figure out why they were losing market share to another manufacturer of domestic power tools. They were particularly concerned about their drills. Despite the very best innovations, they simply weren't selling as well as they should. Jeremy Bullmore spent three weeks talking to the engineers, sales folk, and, most importantly, customers. At the end of his allotted time he met the Board, who were keen to know what was wrong with their drills. "Nothing is wrong with your drills," he reassured them. "But your customers aren't buying drills. They are buying holes."

Black & Decker were fascinated by their machinery, understandably. Their customers, it turns out, were not. The majority of drills were being bought by housewives who were interested in what the machinery could do. If they could have put shelves up or hung that wedding photo another way, they probably would have. The drill was only the means to that end, and no amount of macho claims about multi-speed torque power was going to sway them either way. The clients were crestfallen, but got the message and adapted their marketing accordingly to emphasize ease of use, lightness, and mess-free operation. They had been selling drills. Now they were listening to customers who were buying holes.

The message for anyone who ever sets up a selling meeting is to put yourself in the customers' shoes and figure out what they are buying. Let that be your content.

Whatever you do, if your meeting is about selling—products or plans, a vision or a video player—get on and sell. I once heard an experienced salesman giving words of wisdom to a new recruit who was being hesitantly low key in pitching to a new customer. "You know why you are there. They know why you are there. So BE THERE!" Or else, the moment is going to pass and you'll regret it. Someone's going to walk off with the mammoth meat and you'll be left gnawing the metaphorical bones, as it were.

As Abraham Lincoln memorably put it, *Things may come to those who wait, but only the things left by those who hustle.*

The Meeting for Meeting

"Come over to my cave and talk mammoth?"

People often say that meeting for its own sake is a problem. I absolutely disagree, provided that you are clear about what you are doing in a Meeting for Meeting and why.

The Why of Meetings for Meeting

We are social beings. If we weren't, we'd probably all be self-employed, working at home on our laptops. The fact is, humans have always tended to come together in groups to work. This makes sense economically, logistically, and practically. But we also like company.

The word "Company," which you see in so many business names, reminds us that human enterprises are about the collective effort of *companions*. Businesses happen when two or more people get together and realize they are going to have a richer life if they work together than if they don't.

Other people may drive us nuts at times but, given the choice, most of us would prefer not to work in isolation. Also, it's fun.

And what has fun to do with business? Nothing. Unless you are planning to be the founder of a world-changing tech company ...

I think we're having fun
Steve Jobs

... or an entertainment mogul ...

It's kind of fun to do the impossible
Walt Disney

... or a multi-millionaire, one-man sports franchise

Just play. Have fun. Enjoy the game
Michael Jordan

... or a billionaire entrepreneur

Business has to be involving. It has to be fun
Richard Branson

I often think business is something we humans have invented so we don't get lonely; an excuse to work and play together.

The How of Meetings for Meeting

You can get your company together whenever you want. There is only one time you *must* get them together. And that's when there appears to be no time, no budget, and no good reason. That's when people really appreciate a purely social meeting— and the fact that you're holding one makes them feel appreciated.

Chris, a young Chinese manager working in a cell phone recycling plant in the Phillipines, told me the first time he took his local crew of engineers out for lunch they were dumbstruck. "It was only Kentucky Fried Chicken but no one had ever done that for them. They couldn't figure it out. But because I wasn't after anything other than showing them I appreciated what they were doing, it brought the team together like nothing I have ever seen."

In case you find yourself thinking, this isn't a good return on investment, it's time to remind yourself about the difference between effective and efficient. Having a four-hour, five-course, 16-bottle dinner party for your friends is not very efficient. It takes up a lot of time and leaves you with a hangover, plus calories to burn off in the gym. But who'd want to live in an efficient world without parties?

By the way, if you want to experience a culture where parties are central, hop on a plane to the country of Georgia. The Georgians are the most relentlessly convivial people I have ever met. That is a nation born to party. In the early nineties my opera company went on tour to Tblisi for what I remember as a few performances surrounded by an endless ocean of jollity. In Georgian feasts they don't remove the dishes but pile the next course on top of the old just in case their honored guests aren't completely sated. It got to the point where we would creep back home to the families we were billeted with under cover of darkness and with our shoes off. The slightest creak of a door or flicker of light and the aged grandmother would leap out of bed, uncork a bottle, and start serving food. It was an unforgettable taste of a society that likes to socialize.

The What of Meetings for Meetings

Having been involved in designing and staging hundreds of company events, retreats, conferences, and "offsites," including some very elaborate ones, I'd offer the following three suggestions.

Keep it real

This really goes back to Intent. If you are meeting for the sake (and pleasure) of it, then say that. And do just that. Don't pretend it's work. This is true of the Friday afternoon weekly review which is actually cupcakes and gossip. If that's what the meeting is—call it that. People will appreciate the straightforwardness.

Keep it simple

The simple stuff works. Nice atmosphere. Nice food. Nice drinks. We are sometimes so eager for our teams to have a good time that we over-plan and over-fill the time with "fun." If it's supposed to be relaxing, have the courage to leave as much time in the schedule as you dare empty! You'll find people are quite good at creating their own fun if you let them.

No agenda—not even a hidden one

Anil, a medical research professional I work with, has a natural knack for team building. His key mechanism is a simple meeting which he calls the "Below the Waterline Meeting." It's a monthly meeting, usually held in a bar, where people can talk about anything that's on their mind. And the key reason it is successful is simply this: *no notes*. Anil makes it clear that what is said in this

Meeting for Meeting stays off the record, and there is never, ever any comeback. It is a great way to allow people to put away the professional mask and really meet.

5

MEETING MISCHIEF

"This is all far too important to take seriously"
Ken Campbell

We've looked at the Why of meetings, at the Who, the Where, When, and What. Before you step out there into the Nearly Meeting zone that is the modern world, I want us to talk about How.

How are you going to make the change from nearly meeting to really meeting? And how are you going to make the changes stick? The how is very important, because we have reached a fork in the road.

The traditional way forward, once people have "seen the light" about meetings, is to get all serious and determined about doing things differently. They make commitments. They send emails. They print posters. And after two weeks they give up. Then the How To book goes on the shelf, and life goes on as normal.

If that's your plan, then here's where we part company.

The way ahead is full of skeptics and cynics. People will complain about their meetings but be unwilling to do things differently. They'll agree to your proposals and then forget all about them. They'll appear to adapt to new ideas while clinging on to the old ways for dear life. These are not bad people. They are busy people. You can't rely on their help. Even if you genuinely have their best interests at heart—and I'm sure you do—expect to be operating alone.

It's not going to be enough to be "right." You are going to have to be crafty, cunning, and creative. You are going to have to find artful ways around practical obstacles, be extra playful when others are getting super-professional, meet negativity with enthusiasm, counter heaviness with lightness.

It's not the conventional way. It's certainly not the corporate way. But in my experience, it's going to really help.

Meetings, as we said at the start, are not the sort of subject that has people skipping through their offices with joy. When you try to change meetings you are tampering with the fabric of your business. If the meeting isn't going well, it's usually an indication of something else that is ailing in your organization.

"Meetings aren't the problem—they are symptom of the problem." Bill is a bright, multi-lingual, wise-cracking clinician who knows more than most about symptoms. He stopped me in the corridor to share this with me: "It's like meetings are a microcosm of the macrocosm—fractals of the whole. If a meeting is inefficient then the organisation is inefficient."

The organizational complaint could be serious. But the last thing you want to do is start getting serious, too. Furrowing our brows and getting all determined isn't going to help us here. It will only make the problem more difficult to shift.

In the quotation that starts this chapter, the eccentric theater genius Ken Campbell was reminding us that the more serious you are about an issue, the more solid it becomes.

I hugely admire the people I know who work in NGOs around the world. But they are sometimes so serious about the problems they are tackling (poverty, climate change, youth unemployment, disease) that the problem seems to get progressively vaster. What achievements they do make seem puny by comparison. This can be a real "turn-off" for the public as well as a source of burn-out for NGO workers.

If you get all pushy and put-a-poster-on-the-wall about meetings, you are likely to make matters worse. The more you tell your colleagues they must change, the more they'll dig their heels in. Imagine if a friend of yours kept nagging at you about going on a diet/giving up smoking/seeing "this amazing hypnotherapist they know"; how likely would you be to follow their advice?

Some people are waiting for the meetings to be over for the fun to begin. I say let's have fun with the meetings.

Let's make meeting mischief.

The Change Game means Changing the Game

It's often said that people do not like change. "No one likes a change except a wet baby," goes the phrase. I have found the opposite in the organizations I have worked with. People are desperate for change. Just ask them, "What if this is as good as your life is going to get?" and see the terror in their eyes. Actually no change is far more frightening than change.

What people don't like is "to change." They want the change, just not the process that is required to get there. And that's partly because the change process in companies is so badly done.

Here's the traditional approach:

> *I see something that I don't like and want to change*
> *I make this important*
> *I find others that agree and seek to convert the rest*
> *I do this by identifying what is wrong and offering alternatives*
> *I print these on a poster and/or build a training session around them*
> *I am initially gratified by the results of this process*
> *I am puzzled by the folk who don't seem to "get it," but I am confident they will come around*
> *Life continues. The posters are replaced by other posters. And the change process is duly forgotten*

Let's run that again and take a closer look at what's really happening. I offer my interpretation in italics.

> I see something that I don't like and want to change. *I spot a problem that is happening "out there," forgetting that I may well have some part in creating it.*

> I make this important. *A sure way to make it harder to budge.*

> I find others that agree and seek to convert the rest. *They are not agreeing with you because you are right. It's often just easier to agree than not.*

> I do this by identifying what is wrong and offering alternatives. *This is logical, but who says humans respond to logic?*

> I print these on a poster and/or build a training session around them. *The word training comes from the Latin* trahere, *meaning to drag. Enough said. Posters are helpful in kindergarten, for selling movies, and doctors' offices. And if you think people are not doing what they pledged to do in their training because they don't* remember, *we really do have to talk.*

> I am initially gratified by the results of this process. *This is partly because I hear what I want to. We listen selectively.*

> I am puzzled by the folk who don't seem to "get it," but I hope they will come around. *You don't want to be hoping in an organizational change. If you've ever seen someone standing in the rain at a bus stop, that's what hoping looks like.*

> Life continues. The posters are replaced by other posters. The change process is forgotten. *You get to be proved "right." But nothing really changes.*

This little cartoon strip plays itself out all over the business world. At its heart is a two-part assumption that goes something like this.

> *Things are "going wrong" because people are unaware of what they are doing.*

And

> *Once they become aware of the implications of what they are doing—i.e. by you telling them—they will change.*

It's an approach that runs through organizations like rivers run through canyons. But let's just test that for a moment in real life.

Are we there yet?

Imagine you are on a long car trip. There are two young children in the backseat of the car who are repeatedly kicking the back of your seat. (If you don't have kids, remember what it was like to be one.)

Let's try your traditional change model, the HR tango, to see how well it works.

> Step One: *"Kids. I am not sure you are aware of this but you are kicking the back of my seat."*

They actually knew this already. The kicking continues.

Step Two: *"This is dangerous and distracting and could contribute to the likelihood of us being involved in an accident."*

There is a pause. Then the kicking continues, only now it's harder and more insistent.

What now? Now we parents reach into the glove compartment and bring out the real tools of change:

> **Threat**—*"If you don't stop that YOU ARE WALKING HOME!"*
> **Guilt**—*"OK, keep on kicking me. See if I care."*
> **Bribery**—*"If you stop kicking the seat you can have an ice cream."*
> **Distraction**—*"Hey, is that an ice-cream place in the distance?"*
> **Resignation**—*You just turn up the radio and hope the kicking stops of its own accord.*

Any of the above may work. But I'd like to suggest another gambit: one that's more mischievous and more effective.

Seen through the eyes of the mischief-maker, the kicking of the seat is not a "behavior." It's a game. And the game is called "getting attention."

It is a game we excel at as children. And we carry the skill with us into adult life, especially working life. A lot of the bad behavior that has HR in such a tizzy the world over is actually the Getting Attention Game. And those who play it tend to win.

Think of all that late arrival and interrupting colleagues and all that poor meeting discipline, the politics, the lack of punctuality as a Getting Attention game, and it suddenly makes sense.

There is only one effective way I know to get children to stop playing a game. And that is to replace it with another game. One that is more interesting, more fun, more engaging.

> *"Hey, Kids. I said HEY KIDS! That's a really annoying game you are playing. Let's play a new one. It's called Glue Shoe? The idea is to see who can keep their feet on the car floor the longest. It comes from a story I know (and will tell you when you get quiet) about two young children who meet a Leg Eating Monster in the Forest. It's going to be really fun. The winner gets an ice cream. And the loser WALKS HOME!"*

This particular approach includes getting their attention, stating the facts, offering a bribe, some horror storytelling, a promise, another bribe, and a threat; but essentially it's about substituting one game for another. It doesn't need to be imposed because the children actively choose it.

And to top it off, because the kids know they have won the previous game (getting your attention), they won't lose face by changing to a new one, so it's OK.

I am not saying cultural business change and parenting are the same (parenting is way more challenging), but the parallels are clear.

As with the car trip example, when you are having a lousy meeting, your colleagues are doing the equivalent of kicking the seat because they are getting something from it. You can spend your business life reaching into the back of the car trying to whack them with a rolled-up magazine. *But they will only change when you can come up with a more interesting, attractive alternative.*

Marc Lewis runs a very innovative advertising agency for students called the School of Communication Arts. You'd guess Marc was a Creative (with a big C) from his trademark crazy hair and psychedelic, acid-yellow, skin-tight jeans. You wouldn't necessarily guess he was also a prosperous entrepreneur who is equally at home talking to investors and analysts as he is with advertising types. SCA lives in a funky converted church hall on the South Bank of the River Thames. Every morning begins with an "assembly," and woe betide any student who is late. Marc is big on self-discipline as a pre-requisite for creative success, but being a mischief-maker, Marc has substituted the game of being late (which students excel at in their first term) for the game of creative service.

The day I was there to teach, a cool-looking young art-director-of-the-future walked in a couple of minutes after the morning meeting had started. "Sofa, sofa, sofa" chanted the other students, as Late Guy took up his position facing the class on a squashy pink sofa. The rule is that each of the three next latest students (the previous three to enter the room) now proposes their own "service" that the offender has to perform. And the rest of the students vote for the one they like the most. One student suggested he buy her drinks all night. Another proposed he pose naked for a life drawing class. But the audience finally voted for a week of coffee-making.

I'm guessing the late-comer will be on time for the rest of term (and possibly career). Marc changed the behavior by changing the game. And a really creative game at that!

Another example is what I call Speaker's Corner, after the open-air public-speaking area in London's Hyde Park where anyone can say anything they like. There was a meeting for an insurance company which was increasingly rowdy, with all the participants interrupting each other. You could call the game "The Loudest Wins." It was entertaining in its way to see a clan of alpha males swinging their clubs at each other, but ultimately a real waste of time. One day I brought in a small orange crate and created a new game. The rules were simple: if you have something to say, stand on this box and you will have exactly three uninterrupted minutes to say it. But you have to stay there for three minutes. Two things happened. People stopped shouting because they knew they could be heard if they wanted to be. Those who did use the "Soapbox" quickly found that it's a challenge to fill three minutes of silence in a compelling way. They started becoming more precise, more engaging, more entertaining with their slots, using airtime more effectively.

That was a few years ago and I'm guessing the game petered out long ago. If you want these new rules to stick, you are going to have to get more mischievous yet.

New Games need New Rules

All games, including meeting games, have their rules. If you want to change the game, just change the rules.

If you are a member of the meeting police, you'll create rules for your colleagues and then enforce them (or try to). If you are a meeting mischief maker, you will arrange for your colleagues to create their own new rules and then police themselves!

Here's a way to do this in 20 minutes. And it could save you 20 days this year.

Step One: (1 min)
Explain that as part of the drive for new discipline and decisiveness you are looking to create new agreements for your meeting (you could call them ground rules).

Step Two: (3 min)
Ask the group to consider, "What drives you crazy about our meetings?" Encourage the group to be open and honest. This isn't about blaming individuals but identifying problems. Get a shortlist of at least ten.

Step Three: (1 min)
Now ask them, "Of these, which THREE are we no longer prepared to tolerate?" A simple voting system should provide a Top Three. You can give each person three votes and select the highest scores.

Step Four: (5 min)
Brainstorm ways of avoiding these three.

Step Five: (3 min)

Draw up a contract (example below) which states clearly and positively what you WILL, as a group, COMMIT TO doing differently in your meetings. And for what period of time. We recommend that the new agreement contract lasts for three months. This should be enough time for you to test and refine your new ground rules.

REAL MEETING AGREEMENT

In the interest of effectiveness, satisfaction, professional pride, and personal wellbeing we, the undersigned, no longer tolerate/are now officially "allergic" to the following examples of poor-meeting discipline:

> ....
> ....
> ....

Therefore we agree from (date) to (date) to practice the following with discipline, respect, and good humor:

> ....
> ....
> ....

Signed: ....

Step Six: (2 min)

You finally need to ask everyone to sign the contract. It is amazing how much more powerful commitments are when people physically put their signature on them.

Step Seven: (5 min)

Discuss what you will do when the agreements are, as they probably will be, broken or bent. This is real life, after all. Agreeing how to deal with broken agreements is as important as the agreement itself. If there is no consequence for breaking an agreement, it is not worth much and will quickly be forgotten.

A Great Big Meeting Secret

There is a secret I have learned in my meeting work with organizations. They don't want me to pass this on, which is why I am going to. It is vital you know this if you are going to be effective in creating meeting mischief. So please write it down on a piece of rice paper and eat it afterwards. The secret is this:

Our meetings are bad because we want them to be.

All the "bad" things you say you don't want in your meetings actually give you something. Which is why we accept and keep on doing them. Put it another way, lousy meetings give us something or we wouldn't do them.

If you don't believe me, let's take a look:

WHAT WE SAY WE WANT TO CHANGE	WHAT THESE THINGS ACTUALLY GIVE US
Meetings dominate my day	I have an excuse for not doing anything else. I may not be productive but it's not my fault. As the economist J.K. Galbraith put it: "Meetings are indispensible when you don't want to do anything"
Meetings are boring	I get to feel so much more interesting than the people around me
Meetings are indecisive	If we delay the decision we delay the risk of maybe getting it wrong
People don't say what they mean	I don't have to either. It may be suboptimal but it's safer
Meetings are poorly prepared	I have an excuse for turning up unprepared myself. Lack of preparation saves me time
Meetings are dominated by others	I get to keep a low profile
Meetings are divisive and cliquey	It's nice to feel part of a clan
Meetings drive me crazy	Anger is a powerful emotion. I get to feel angry. And righteously so. This makes me (seem) a more interesting, powerful, and attractive person. I am a hero

So it's a great idea, before you start changing meetings, to ask your colleagues: *what do we get from keeping them as they are?*

It's not going to make you popular, at least not at the start. The thing about complaints, particularly in organizations, is that they are a wonderful way of bringing people together, to bond around a common grouse. So when people moan, they will expect you to agree; *yes, meetings are a real pain; no, they'll never change; no, it's not our fault.*

When you throw them a curveball question like this you are challenging the accepted view of the world; shaking it like a big fat quivering bowl of Jello. It's mischievous and effective.

As Richard Bandler, the originator of Neuro Linguistic Programming (NLP) put it, *"You can change the world or you can change your model of the world. One is a lot easier than the other."*

Here's an example of basic NLP that shows what we mean by changing the model.

A friend comes to you in tears, having broken up with their partner. "I'll never love again," they wail. You have two choices.

Choice A is to be a Shoulder to Cry On. You say "poor you" and "there, there" and "it must feel awful." It's sympathetic, but you haven't challenged the central assumption. In fact you are tacitly agreeing, confirming their model of the world. Poor Destined-to-be-Alone Them.

Choice B is to shoot back a curveball question like, "When you say never, do you mean never-ever-ever? Or will you love again in a few years' time?" You just rocked the model. It's not what your friend expected—or perhaps even wanted—to hear. Their model of the world at the moment is of eternal singleness. Misery requires it. You can't get really upset if you think the pain of lost love is a temporary phenomenon. Chances are the misery will dry up and in half an hour you'll be downing cocktails talking about there being "plenty more fish in the sea." The question you ask the sufferer can create more suffering. Or less.

Other Curveball Model Wobblers

So what about the "meeting sufferer"? For the times when you are at work and someone says to you (or indeed you say to yourself) a simple "true" statement like "My meetings are lousy and will never change," here are a few curveball questions you can throw back that shake that way of thinking about the problem and make it easier to maneuver:

1. *All of your meetings?* (get them to be specific)
2. *When you say "my," do you mean the ones you attend, the ones you lead, or both?* Watch out for how often people feel all the meetings they lead are OK, but all the ones they attend are not. If this is true—and it's a little unlikely—then ask them "why aren't you teaching your colleagues how to make the bad ones better?"
3. *"Lousy" how?* (be specific)
4. *Is it just you who thinks this?* (are we talking opinion or fact?)
5. *Do the meetings really need to change?* (are better meetings nice-to-have or must-have?)
6. *Change how?* If they had changed for the better how would they look?

And, finally, the model killer:

7. *What do you get out of them being exactly as lousy as you say they are?*

They may not thank you initially. But which would you rather be? A shoulder to cry on, or a life-changing colleague? The choice is yours.

Breaking the Bad Meeting Habit

Meetings are bad not because we are bad people. We are good people who have fallen into bad habits.

You don't get poor discipline, lousy communication, catastrophically bad preparation, deep disrespect, and profound boredom without adequate practice. It takes time for meetings to get truly awful.

What you need to remember when you are out there trying to change things is that *all bad habits had "good" reasons once.*

As illogical as a habit may seem, it usually has a logical foundation. To change a habit you need to understand its rational source, and that may mean returning to the time when it *all* made perfect sense.

Consider smoking, a habit that many would like to kick. Cigarette packs luridly remind us that smoking is an illogical thing to do. But go back to the time when the average smoker started lighting up and there was a "good" reason for it. It was a way to look good, feel good, be accepted, take a risk, show the world your independence from parental control, etc. Part of the therapeutic journey of the "recovering smoker" is to recognize that (a) smoking was indeed logical once and (b) that logic has now been outgrown.

Try this with meetings. The procedure that makes no sense to you now was once very sensible. Ask yourself what this procedure intended to achieve. Do we still need to do this? And if so, is there a more efficient way?

A lot of those information-sharing meetings fall under this category. *Was this logical once?* Certainly, there was a time before email, fax or even telex when a face-to-face download made a lot of sense. How else would you know what other members of your team or group had been up to? *Is this still useful?* Yes. *But is there a better way of doing it?* Yes. Because the technology now exists to share important information *outside* a meeting, we don't need the meeting any more. If you have CNN, why would you wait to get your news from a town crier who comes to your door with a big bell? The old habit was legitimate. But now, let's move on.

Leadership team meetings at Skandia used to be dominated by information sharing. Today the board circulates detailed information in advance and in the meeting handles only *questions arising from the information*. The "sharing" habit has become a "diagnostic" habit. We have moved on.

Remember, we are all to some extent addicted. Assailing us with logic only makes us hide our habits under the bed. Much better to admit there is a logic to what we are doing, offer an alternative, and let the addict make the choice.

BMA (Bad Meeting Addiction)

As an agent of change you may run into an even deeper form of unhealthy meeting habit—*meeting addiction*.

Dr. Wayne Dwyer, the popular physician and speaker, says you know you are addicted "when you can't get enough of what you don't want." It's a definition that certainly applies to nearly meetings. We know they are bad for us but we continue to bloat our diaries with them in an endless bad-meeting binge.

Again, it's helpful—and mischievous—to search for the central logic which enables this addiction to make sense to the addict. As a nice illustration Richard Bandler, the maverick creator of NLP, was once asked to treat an "incurable" psychiatric patient who was convinced he was Jesus. Doctors had tried and failed to persuade the patient that pretending you are the Savior of Mankind is simply illogical. Bandler's approach was rather different. He bought a saw, two huge beams, and a box of nails. He set up his sawhorse by the patient's bed and got to work, whistling merrily. "What are you doing?" asked the patient. "Building you a Cross, Master," said Bandler. Those who have met Richard Bandler will understand why the patient would have been convinced he meant business. The patient began to have second thoughts and before long he was desperately trying to convince Bandler that he was *not* Jesus after all. Rather than attacking the patient's logic, Bandler embraced it, and the logical consequences of maintaining it. The patient now had simply to choose between one logic and a less inconvenient/painful one.

In another example, my father used to lead a Mental Health Tribunal in the U.K. to assess whether or not patients could be released from the hospital. He frequently received letters from patients claiming they had been unjustly detained and laying out their reasons why. These letters were often in extraordinary detail, bulging out of their envelopes and written with luridly colored pens. My dad called them his "green ink" letters. He kept them in a separate pile and gave them special attention. I wondered why he didn't just put them in the garbage and he explained; *"They may be disturbed, but it doesn't mean they are not right."* In the interests of justice, my father was prepared to step into their logic rather than simply judge from his.

Understanding the underlying logic of behavior, however bizarre or annoying, is a key to busting the bad meeting habits in your business.

Another powerful technique derives from the mountains of Tibet.

Advanced Habit Busting

The Tibetan Buddhists have an inspired approach to changing behavior which they call, rather mysteriously, *water out of your ear by means of water in your ear.*

The idea is to cure a habit by doing it deliberately. Habits are automatic thinking. The same signal has traveled down the same neural pathways so often they now do this without our conscious awareness. In order to change the habit, you first have to reclaim that part of your mind that is now on autopilot. You do this by deliberately doing the unwanted activity until your poor brain actually realizes what it has been automatically doing. Becoming conscious gives you control again. And you can make a new choice. Or not.

How does this apply to meetings?

Punctual Lateness

A team complained to me that their leader was always late for meetings. I had a word and discovered she was late for all her meetings, not just this one, and was feeling bad about it. It was a habit she wanted to kick but didn't know how. I put her on a strict regime of deliberate lateness for a week. She had to turn up everywhere exactly twelve and a half minutes late. It was agony for her. Partly because, as the week went on and she became more aware of her timekeeping, she actually started turning up early and had to waste time for her regulation twelve and a half minutes to pass. By the end of the week those automated "lateness" synapses were back under new management and she had a choice about whether to be on time or not.

Make Dull Meetings Duller

Another candidate for this mischievous form of habit busting is our friend the Dull Meeting. A good analogy is with boiling frogs slowly so they don't notice the heat increasing. Meetings get progressively dull over time, so we don't notice we are incrementally lowering our standards. We begin to feel that graveyard dull meetings (and that's being rude to graveyards) are the norm.

If you want to make your meetings interesting, you could first make them duller to wake up the participants.

WILL THERE BE DONUTS?

It's a lesson I learned from the great Nina Simone on one memorable evening at Ronnie Scott's jazz club in London's Soho. The room was crammed with middle-class folk (like me) who were high on expectation but not necessarily the most loose-hipped audience the jazz diva had ever played to.

We had come prepared to listen to a concert. She had come to play a vibrant jazz "gig" and was clearly not impressed. Stone-faced, she played an interminable, dirge-like blues while the audience nodded along, eyes closed, smiling to themselves. Then she played another, even slower and more mournful. And another. At the end of that one (and it couldn't have come too soon) she fixed us with a baleful eye. "And they're *all* going to be like that tonight—unless you start to enjoy yourselves." Point well made, we all loosened up, started to chat, laugh, talk, and have a good time.

To wake up your meetings à la Nina Simone, list the five most boring things about them and then plan them in. Really go for it. How dull can you make the PowerPoint? How much superfluous detail can you include? How technical can you make your language? How lifeless can you make the room? (A dead pot plant could help.) How gray can your shirt be? You get the idea. So will they. You will know that the message has hit home when someone else asks you if they can "jazz up this meeting" a little. Mission accomplished. Allow yourself an inner smile.

One Fine Meeting

If you want to take this further, try an idea I call "One Fine Meeting." This not only benefits your meetings but also your chosen charity. The idea is simple. You draw up a list of meeting *don'ts* that you all wish to avoid. You agree that every time one of these is broken the perpetrator pays a "fine" to charity. You are raising awareness and cash at the same time. Clients love this game, actively competing to see who can out-bore the other or answer the most illicit mails in a meeting. And the better (i.e. worse) they play, the more they pay.

A Menu of Charges can be fun:

> *Lateness—$10*
> *Bad PowerPoint—$25*
> *Overrunning your slot—$10*
> *Pontificating—$50*
> *Speaking over others—$5*
> *Side-talking—$5*
> *Covert emailing/BlackBerry—$10*
> *Turning up unprepared—$50*
> *Bad jokes—$5–$50 (depending on how bad)*
> *Wearing "that tie" again—penalty payment to be determined by your colleagues*

It's a cheeky, compassionate, competitive, and consciousness-raising way to improve your meetings. Plus, a "sin list" like this can also be a useful way to keep meeting discipline on your radar in future.

I think of techniques like these as Meeting Homeopathy. Just as a modest amount of poison awakens the body and its defenses, so a little bit of extra meeting misbehavior gets your meetings working much more healthily.

Keep or Kill?

There are lots of people out there who have no time for the "soft stuff." They think of themselves as hard-nosed pragmatists. I can spot them a mile off and know that their eyes will glaze over the moment I start talking about the power of real meetings, being human at work, or simply communicating better. If you challenge their right to hold an ineffective meeting but don't have the appropriate language to make your case, they won't engage.

So I have created an exercise which talks directly to their logic. They love it. And it really helps when you want to work out which meetings to keep and which to kill.

It's a kind of investment game, which I call the Black Box Test.

Imagine a meeting is a black box, one designed to convert energy into value. You put energy in one side. That's the sum total of time, effort, attention, cash invested for everyone to prepare for, take part in, and follow up the meeting. Value emerges from the other. That's not just the meeting's value for you, by the way, but the sum total for everyone involved. For the team. For the organization as a whole.

Now it's simple. If you are putting more energy IN than value is coming OUT, it's a poor investment. I call it a SINK meeting. It's draining your resources. You could reduce the investment and try to increase the output. But I suggest you kill the meeting. No one will miss it. If it really needs to happen you'll quickly know. And you can design a new one from scratch.

If the energy going IN is the same as the value coming OUT, it's also poor investment. It's not really an investment at all. It's Steady State; what I call a SLEEPER meeting that's actually going nowhere. Kill it. This may not be as easy, because it doesn't scream out for change. It's more like a slow leak than a flat tire. But kill it nevertheless, or at least downgrade it until you come up with a better place to invest your time.

Clearly, that leaves the meeting which radiates more value OUT than the energy you put IN. The SOLAR meeting, I like to call it. I'd argue this is the only kind of meeting you should be having. The additional refinement is further to reduce input and increase output, so the meeting becomes both even more effortless and even more value-creating.

My clients love the black box process. It quickly identifies those meetings whose intentions have nothing to do with creating value. The notion of Meeting ROI (return on investment) gives a nice unemotional basis for culling meetings.

You may find it hard to be precise about the value a meeting generates. If you do, here are four ways around the problem:

> *If you want to assess the value of the output for those taking part, ask them.*
> *If you can't assess the value you are generating by having the meeting, see if you can identify the value that will be lost if you don't have the meeting.*
> *If you can't be accurate, then make a reasonable guess.*
> *If you genuinely can't assess monetary value, then agree on another unit of measurement. Morale units, perhaps.*

If none of these works, I'd suggest it's not that the output *cannot* be valued but that people do not *want* to value it. Your colleagues and your business would rather not know the ROI because it is going to lay bare the fact that you have a laughably poor meeting investment portfolio. That's embarrassing for your hard-nosed business types and really encourages them to make changes.

Whatever the reason, if you are attending a meeting where the return on your investment is unknown, you certainly do have to wonder if this is a meeting worth investing in.

Value your time

The investment approach also reminds people that their time is valuable and that it is theirs to invest. Or it should be.

Modern though they look, many enterprises are stuck in a feudal time-bubble where the boss owns your time. OK, perhaps feudal is a bit unfair. The boss is unlikely to steal your livestock or sleep with your daughter on her wedding night, but it's a fairly medieval system nonetheless. A sort of hidden serfdom.

A lot of the static you'll encounter when you start unpicking the meeting conventions in your business is, I believe, rooted in the feeling that participants can't control their own time. Because they don't decide which meetings they do and don't attend, their attendance doesn't mean a lot. If you can't say no to an invitation, there is no power in saying yes.

Powerless people tend to have powerless meetings.

This is a situation that takes two—or more—to tango. For slavery to be perpetuated, people have to behave like slaves. Often, when more junior people say, "I have to attend," they actually mean something like, "I think I have to attend but I don't have the courage to find out and/or challenge the usefulness of me being here when I fear I might lose my job if I did."

"The bosses" are often made the baddy in this situation. Sometimes that is deserved, but often it is just poor communication. Senior people are not especially psychic, at least not the ones I have met and worked with. If you want to challenge your attendance at a meeting, it is helpful to let them know what's on your mind.

If you are not a serf, but are acting like one, cut it out. Or stop complaining.

But what if you are the other half of the problem? The Robber Baron of a boss who is stealing everyone's time? Of course, you don't feel like one. But it doesn't mean that isn't how people see you or how you function in the organization.

Hero or Villain?

When clients complain to me that their life seems dull and routine, I'll introduce them to the Hero's Journey. This is an age-old formula upon which great stories—and pretty much all Hollywood movies—are built. It helps people rethink their "ordinary" lives as a story with themselves as its central hero. Suddenly adventure is possible. Small events gain epic significance. There are trials to face and opponents to overcome. This doesn't make the routine go away—but it does become much more interesting.

Very few of us are brought up to think of ourselves as heroes. So it can be a stretch for adult professionals to see themselves as having the central role in their own story. But, with a little practice, you get the hang of it. When you start seeing every business day through the protagonist's "viewfinder," there's no such thing as a dull moment.

This can work very well with meetings. Every meeting becomes a scene with a direction, something to achieve, something to learn.

One important caveat, however—and it can be a shock—is this:

> *While you are playing the hero in your own story, you may well be playing the villain in someone else's.*

It doesn't mean you are a baddy in the obvious sense, or that you mean ill to others. It's just that, while you may see others as an adversary, they may think precisely the same about you.

So here's a test. As you are reading this book, are you concentrating on the meetings which are a difficulty for you? Or the meetings that you are making difficult for others?

Is it just possible that for others in the business the meeting problem *is* YOU?

Is it possible that:

> ❯ *when you take the limelight, "they" feel pushed into the shadows?*
> ❯ *what you find fascinating "they" find irrelevant?*
> ❯ *when you are looking for consensus, "they" see lack of decisiveness?*
> ❯ *when you invite them to share ideas "they" think you want to steal them?*

Is it possible that, wonderful as we know you are, they may be thinking these negative things about you? And that they might be right?!

The meetings you don't see as a problem, others might. And the problem might be one you are contributing to, or even creating.

The length and breadth of the business world, people are blaming each other for the meetings they are having. Not themselves. I am told it is the boss's fault. Or the rank and file. Or the senior management. Or the system. It's always them, them, them.

And if we are going to change things, someone is going to have stop the buck. Let's start now.

Get Feedback from Others

One way to discover if you are part of the problem is to ask for feedback at the end of a meeting. Not a bland "How did that go?" You'll get an equally bland "OK" in return.

You could try something like:

> *"As you know, I am determined to improve the quality of this meeting by leading it better. Personally, I'd rate that [six] out of ten. What do you think?"*

Give Yourself Feedback

A second technique—more tricky but much more fun—is to give yourself your own feedback using a simple process that I call *"If that were true I'd..."*

You simply imagine the meeting from their point of view. Literally swivel your memory round so you are seeing yourself through the eyes of the other attendees. From this position, if you see anything that you don't like about what you said or did in the meeting, and/or that could be improved, note it down.

If you've been honest you should now have two or three points to consider. If you have a much longer list, I suspect you are being super-self-critical and I suggest you lie down until this bout of perfectionism passes.

I don't know about you, but when I get feedback my first instinct is to justify myself. Despite my attempts to control this, I usually think I am right and/or misunderstood. Or rather my ego does. And inside my head it is shouting, *"Fair point, but ..."*, or *"I see where you are coming from, but ..."*, or *"If your life was a difficult and challenging as mine you'd understand that ..."*

Put that voice on hold if you can and simply respond to each point by completing the sentence *If that were true I'd ...*

For example, standing outside myself and seeing me in a meeting from someone else's viewpoint, I might think: "David makes the point but keeps talking ..." or "David didn't talk about what interests me—sales ..." or "What is the deal with David's shirt? It looks like a chameleon threw up on it ..."

When I place these pieces of imagined feedback into the mix, it generates useful improvements to try out:

"David makes the point but keeps talking ..."
*If that were true I'd ... check with the audience they have received
    the message and then move on to the next point*

"David didn't talk about what interests me—sales ..."
If that were true I'd ... give prominence to sales next week

"What is the deal with David's shirt? It looks like a chameleon
threw up on it ..."
*If that were true I'd ... listen to my kids, admit it was a mistake and
wear a nice plain pullover?*

The Accountability Thing

While you are out there in the wild, hunting Nearly Meetings to
fell and turn into Really Meetings, I want you to do me a favor.

I want you to think of any and every meeting you attend as
your meeting. You may be running it. You may be participating.
You may be attending and not actively participating. You may be
on the end of a phone in Kuala Lumpur. If you are in the meeting,
it's no longer theirs, it's yours. You have a stake in its success. You
have a responsibility for its outcome.

Why do I say this? Do I want to heap more work onto your
shoulders? No. I want to put more energy in your tank, more
spring in your step, more power in your elbow.

I want you to stop acting like a victim of meetings—victims
just get victimized more—and start thinking of yourself as
accountable for them.

The simplest way to switch is to start actively choosing. The
minute you say to yourself, *"I choose to be in this meeting,"* the
creativity, power, self-respect, and possibilities return.

It's a tip I picked up in the theater. You can feel pretty
powerless in theater, very much at the mercy of an unknown

audience that you barely see out there in the dark. It's easy to feel a victim. So, on arriving in a new venue, I used to walk around it, looking at the stage and auditorium, while in my mind I'd be saying, like a mantra, "I choose to be in this theatre, the stage is just as I would have wanted it. The audience that is coming is the perfect audience. I choose this experience!" The stage hands thought I was weird, but it worked for me. By the end I had double the confidence and three times the energy for the performance.

The effect of "I choose" is particularly powerful when you have no real choice.

While an inmate of Theresienstadt, the psychologist Victor Frankl observed that the people most likely to survive in a concentration camp were those who thought and acted like they had choice—even though the regime had actually deprived them of any say in their future. Those who felt truly powerless in the situation more often perished. It's a dramatic lesson we can all learn from.

The statement "I have no choice" is both factually untrue and utterly corrosive to the success of any enterprise. What chances would you give a marriage which had "I have no choice" as its motto? How happy are customers who feel they are obligated to stay with a supplier, held hostage by tricksy sales techniques or complex hidden clauses that "make you stay with them"?

"My husband made me crash the family car," said a tight-jawed woman executive in a recent session I was holding on Accountability. She was clearly still furious. I asked her to restart the sentence with the words "I chose to crash the family car ..."

She was initially very reluctant. Then, despite herself, her face cracked into a smile of inner knowing.

"I chose to crash the family car because I wanted to show my husband how distracting it is for him to talk on and on and on about his work while I am driving without once asking me *how my day went ...*"

This had the ring of truth about it. The simple act of choosing put her, quite literally, in the driving seat of that particular experience. She wasn't a mute, complaining victim, but a choice-making player.

And that's how I want you to feel in even the most awful, hopeless meeting. *This is my meeting.*

I choose this awful meeting because:

> *there is so much wrong with it, I have endless opportunities to learn new skills*
> *it sharpens my desire for great meetings*
> *I am not going to let my colleagues suffer alone*
> *I have to change things from the inside*
> *if I can change this one, I can change any*

Every meeting is YOUR meeting.

The Buck Stops Where?

The Accountability attitude not only makes you feel like a more empowered human, it makes you more capable and willing to lead. The simple and golden rule of accountability is *we take care of what's ours.*

Management Consultant Ron puts it succinctly when he says: "If you look around and there's no one else taking the leadership, the leader is you." He admits being accountable in this way isn't always convenient, but he says it is strategically helpful. "I'll often ask myself do I want to take the buck here? Then I remember it may be painful now but could be very useful further down the way."

Stepping in when others are wavering can also be tactically powerful. Particularly at the end of the meeting ...

He Who Summarizes, Wins

There is a commandment that Moses didn't write down, though given the difficulty he had in his meetings with those discordant tribes of Israel, he probably should have. It goes thus:

THOU SHALT OWN THE SUMMARY

You probably think that the job of summing up the meeting is to record what happened. Wrong. If you are practicing meeting mischief, the real job of summing up is to record what you want people to *remember* happened. And to *direct* what happens next. Back to consultant Ron, who confesses, with a twinkle in his eye,

> *If you take control of the summing up, you take control of the meeting. Typically, I will step in and say something like, "We don't have much time so let me just recap." I will then highlight the points I really want people to hold on to. While I am giving them my take on what has happened, I'll also*

weave in what I feel should happen next. "And as we said, I'm going to do a, b, c, and you're going to do x, y, z." We call it synthesizing but it's actually taking control, leading.

Back Office or Bust

If the meetings are the stage of modern business, then the back office is backstage. And as you quickly learn in the performing arts, the people backstage can make or break your performance.

Quite literally "break." At the end of Puccini's opera *Tosca* the lead soprano flings herself from her death off the battlements—in fact falling onto a mattress below. One Australian diva was so hoity-toity with a stage manager that he substituted a trampoline and the unfortunate woman was hilariously bounced back into the audience's view several times before bouncing off and breaking her collar-bone. It could be a myth. I hope it isn't.

The stage management, production crew, and technical staff are the connective tissue and nervous system of any great show. They are not in the limelight, but without them nothing happens.

This is why, when a company asks me to help them change their meeting culture, I ask to spend a lot of time with PAs, secretaries, and other so-called back office staff. They are actually the front-liners in meeting-making. They manage the diaries, send and accept invitations, book rooms, take minutes, order the donuts. They can be an exceptionally powerful force in moving organizations—particularly large ones—from *nearly* to *really* meeting.

I was talking to a group of local government clerks recently. They fulfill the PA/minute-taking role in the thousands of U.K.

council meetings held every year. They were desperate to make changes, but it's a hierarchical system they work in and they see their position as a relatively lowly one. "How many of you are allowed to change how meetings are run?" I asked. No one put their hand up. Technically they are right. None of them has the mandate to redesign meetings. My next question was "How many of you can influence how meetings are run?" And almost everyone put their hand up. They knew how impactful a well-timed comment in the busy chairwoman's ear can be, or a helpful little suggestion to a stressed chairman. That's the back office: not powerful, perhaps, but highly influential.

A successful meeting revolution is going to benefit support staff as much as those they support. Here are some practical ways to collaborate:

> *Be creative about meeting timings. When meetings both start and end on the hour, those taking part are doomed to be arriving late or leaving early. A meeting hour is never an hour of meeting. You need to allow time to arrive and a clear zone at the end for people to make it to their next meeting (should they be unlucky enough to have back-to-back meetings). Those who manage diaries and room bookings can help enormously by, for example, ending all meetings at "ten to the hour." I know PAs who do this* and *turn up at the meeting to make sure their executive doesn't overrun. Saying "Your taxi's waiting" with a pointed stare tends to work.*

> *Make a contract with your assistant, if you have one, to hold you to your agreements. If you say, for example, that you will*

not accept an invitation unless it includes a clear intention for the meeting, then empower your assistant to say NO and mean it. Once you have given them this power, do not undercut it by accepting a meeting they have declined. You will be back to square one in a moment.

> *While you are at it, empower them to challenge you about the meetings you choose to hold and/or attend. Have a conversation with them (quarterly) in which you explain your priorities, and ask for their help in insuring you keep to these. Many of the most successful people I know have someone standing between their diaries and the outside world—a gatekeeper—whose job is to filter every request.*

> *And remember, it is not just the senior person's time that is precious.*

"I am amazed that junior people in an organization don't consider their time as valuable as a senior person's," says consultant Ron. "It's like junior time is an infinite commodity. Junior people often rush around making sure they get the absolute best out of the boss's limited time, but they treat their own time as if it's worth nothing. I think they should imagine that at 5 p.m. they will vaporize. That should remind them to get the most out of their day."

> *Assistants, you should create meeting-free zones in the day and make sure your executives leave the office on time. If people feel the day is endlessly elastic, meetings will drag on and they will be at the office forever.*

❯ *Don't ask for notes to be taken or minutes to be written unless you are going to use them. My heart goes out to the assistants I see hauling a pile of flipcharts and Post-it notes out of a meeting room. I imagine the only thing worse than spending hours deciphering lots of management scribble and committing this to PowerPoint is the certain knowledge that no one is going to read any of it.*

When the Going Gets Tough—Keep Going!

One of the biggest challenges you'll face "out there" in nearly meeting land is stamina. You're going to need to bounce through stuck and clogged situations with the irrepressible zing of a turbo-charged Tigger. You'll be like a meeting plumber who's on call 24/7 with your plunger and dynorod at the ready to blast through communication blockages and to scoop turgid conventions out of the organizational U-bend. Dead or dying meetings suck your energy like a vampire. How and where are you going to replace it?

As the final gift of this section I'd like to offer you some techniques and tools which you can use to sustain and build your energy while you are living on your wits behind "enemy lines." Think of them as the dried berries and nutritional road kill of the Meeting Survival game.

How do you keep really connecting when it's the last thing you want to do?

"Hell is other people," said Jean-Paul Sartre. And a few weeks into your Real Meeting campaign you'll probably sympathize. I love my fellow man (and woman). I really do. Why else would I dash around the world meeting, working with, and hopefully inspiring them? That doesn't mean I always *like* them. Let's face it, at close quarters other people can be irritating, maddening, infuriating.

How are you going to find the energy to connect with them, when all you want to do is cover your head with a blanket and play Nintendo for the day? There will be times when you are going to lose interest. When that happens, get curious.

Curiosity is the most powerful generator of connective energy I have ever come across. But don't listen to me. I'm a cuddly, arty, connective type. Listen to a hard-headed corporate Titan. We'll call him Angus.

Angus had a small but significant problem. He'd describe himself as "an operational guy." His passion was setting up, managing, and completing large and complex engineering projects. As COO of a major engineering company, that was only to be expected. Except now the COO was being groomed by the board to be CEO. And as a CEO Angus would have to be more of a "people person." This was a problem.

He was well enough liked and deeply respected by people who knew and worked with him. It was the others that were tricky. People that Angus met for the first time found him a bit distant, preoccupied, cut off. That's exactly how he felt, particularly at cocktail parties and networking events where a CEO is expected to thrive. "*I loathe these events,*" he confided to me. "*I've got no time for the chit-chat. Not unless the people I am meeting are germane to the business.*" If you were in a social gathering with Angus, you'd see him efficiently "working the room," checking off the business-relevant people, and then he'd lurk in the corner or leave.

Like many of us, Angus wasn't a natural connector type. Basically an introvert, he didn't thrive in the social aquarium. And he found it difficult to connect with people he didn't know or find interesting.

You don't have to be a high-flier to experience this problem. Every time you find yourself in a meeting—live or virtual—you're probably going to be called on to make a connection with other people you don't know, don't find interesting, or don't especially like.

People pick this up. More than you'd imagine. And this can only create difficulties. But what are you to do? You're just a human being, after all, with a limit to your energy and ability to connect.

Here's where I'd recommend curiosity. As I did to Angus on the eve of a particularly important industry networking event full of the uninteresting people he dreaded meeting.

Curiosity is one of the most powerful ways I have found to make and sustain connection with others. It's wonderfully democratic. Interest requires people to be interesting. You can be curious about anyone.

You can be sitting across the table from someone who doesn't interest you at all and still be curious about where they come from, what makes them tick, why they chose that shirt, what they had for breakfast.

When you direct that kind of curious attention onto other people, this communicates. And creates instant rapport.

I am writing this in a hotel in Liguria which I booked as I thought it would be a good way to write without being distracted by people. As if ...

You can tell it's a swanky hotel because they have a chef available to produce a custom-made breakfast omelette for you. I was lining up this morning and I noticed that the guests before me and after me in the line both simply asked the cook for fried eggs. I asked her how many omelettes she had made that day. I wasn't being fresh, just curious. And suddenly it wasn't a transaction, but a meeting; only two minutes long, but a real meeting nevertheless. Now I know her name (Alessandra) where she came from (Rome), how many kids she has (one son), how crazy he drives her (very), why she was working in the hotel (tuition costs) and what job she really wanted to do (dressmaker). I also picked up a phrase of native Roman dialect (unrepeatable here) and, in case you were curious, the number of omelettes she'd made that day was 120; 121 including mine. Curiosity had turned a functional moment into an experience. I was richer for it and I swear my eggs tasted better.

To his surprise, curiosity worked for Angus, too. I suggested he use the words "I am curious about ..." to start off those usually awkward conversations. It felt artifical at first, stilted. But as the evening wore on he noticed that it did the trick. He met more people. And some of those initially uninteresting people turned out to be potential customers (something that should interest a CEO a lot). What's more, though he was shy about admitting it, Angus actually enjoyed it.

Curiosity is a secret battery you can tap into in your meetings. It powers up your senses, gets your imagination working, breaks down barriers, effortlessly starts connecting you with other participants. It is particularly effective in virtual meetings.

Curiosity makes connections across time-zones quicker than electrons down a broadband cable.

One leader I coached was going through a particularly bumpy patch with the leader of his South American franchise. Every call was getting more difficult and volatile. One day I intercepted my client a few minutes before he picked up the BlackBerry and suggested he spend a few moments being curious about Eduardo, rather than annoyed. *What's on his mind? What's in his back pocket? What's the humidity like in the room where he's working? What's it like to be him today?* Sounds crazy, but their calls improved immediately.

Curiosity is powerful because it makes you notice rather than think.

POCs Rock

Routine has its uses, but too much of it is going to drain energy out of you. Routine meetings beget routine thinking. The minute you say to yourself a meeting is *always like this*, you're more than half-way to making that a foregone conclusion.

Meetings, even *regular* meetings, don't have to be *routine* ones if you are prepared to approach them fresh every time. But how do you do that when, try as you might, it's that dreaded Thursday afternoon sales meeting *again*?

One way, which I encountered originally in the theater, is to give yourself a Point of Concentration or POC.

As a member of the audience you want to feel that the show you are seeing is being done for the first time. It needs to feel fresh and immediate. This is something of a challenge to the performers, who may be getting on stage for the 300th time. A technique we use to keep things alive is to give ourselves a Point of Concentration for that show, something we'll concentrate on—in the background, as it were—while we do our performance. For example:

> *Tell the story*
> *Accentuate the emotions*
> *It's winter*
> *The audience speaks a foreign language so you have to be super clear*
> *I am hot (either temperature or sexual attractiveness would work)*
> *Listen carefully*
> *Concentrate on the third toe of my left foot*

Simple and odd instructions like this (the odder the better) force the performer out of their routine and prompt them to do things slightly differently. This newness communicates itself to the audience and the show feels more spontaneous.

It works exactly the same in meetings. Before you go into a regular meeting, you can say to yourself, "In this meeting I am going to ...

> *Really listen*
> *Notice the color of things*
> *Focus on my breathing*

> *See the funny side*
> *Concentrate on the third toe of my left foot"*

There's another, naughtier technique for zapping a dull meeting with energy. If you get into trouble using this, I shall deny ever having mentioned it!

The Secret Game

I first saw this as a rehearsal technique. If there's a scene which is getting stale, the performers stuff dishcloths down their pants, leaving a "tail" hanging down behind. (If you are doing this in front of a live audience, handkerchiefs are more discreet and work just as well.) As you play the scene you try to whip the dish-cloth out of your colleague's pants without the audience noticing, so winning a point. I have seen dull scenes start to sizzle as the Countess bears down on the retreating Vicar with "dishcloth mania" in her eye. The audience isn't aware of the game, only of the energy that it generates as a by-product. And that's the point. The secret game energizes the players and infuses the ordinary with excitement.

I don't recommend the dishcloth thing in a live meeting, but simpler versions work well. Here's my friend Ron in confessional mood:

> *One of my very senior clients would always weave lyrics*
> *from eighties' pop songs into meetings. Even very serious*
> *meetings. You can imagine the situation. References about*
> *"when the going gets tough," or that the competition are "on*

a road to nowhere," and how the restricted information is "for your eyes only" and we mustn't be careless about who we whisper it to. It was never mentioned, but those of us in the know were on tenterhooks.

There was a scoring system where you got one point for noticing the lyric but you'd lose two if it made you crack up or miss a beat in your presentation. Surreptitiously, whoever was at the white board would be marking up the score, disguised in a chart or diagram. The other participants were oblivious to the game and it never derailed a meeting. In fact, it had the opposite effect. It sharpened our listening and got us really paying attention. Even dull meetings became fun.

But there's another, more profound way that you can hit the refresh button, not only in your meetings but throughout your life.

If there's a boring meeting, don't go. Send another you.

"Know thyself!" said the Greek philosopher Plato, arguing that you couldn't understand the world unless you really understood yourself. Today, I suggest, it would be more appropriate to say, *"Know thyselves."*

Thanks to breakthroughs in psychology, neurology, and cognitive science, we've been proved to be much more complex beings than previously thought. It turns out we don't have a single intelligence but many.

WILL THERE BE DONUTS?

We are less a lump and more a clump—not a unified whole but a diverse collection of different elements working together. It's like a car where no one driver is in charge, but different parts of yourself take over the wheel at different times and in different contexts.

One of the things I like about my life is the variety of different mes I get to play in a normal day. Husband, Dad, Friend, Commuter, Professional, Businessman, Consumer, Coach, Performer, Musician, Wiseguy, Idiot.

I think of this as my repertoire, the mes I use most often. We all have a repertoire, a potentially huge one. Buddhists maintain there are 10,000 selves within us waiting for a "turn" at the steering wheel.

Building your repertoire of "selves" and using them frequently is, I believe, key to making our meetings—and our entire lives—much more interesting than they are at present.

To see what I mean, please jot down five versions of yourself you use most commonly at the moment. Go on, do it now.

Now add five personalities (aka aspects of yourself) you'd like to be more often. I call them "persions"—a cross between personalities and versions.

So you now have doubled your repertoire. It's like having ten cards in your back pocket and you can play any one of them. Some clients actually do draw these "persions" out on cards and carry them around so they'll remember this technique.

Before you begin a meeting (on the way there, in the corridor, in the 15 seconds before you pick up the phone) ask yourself:

MEETING MISCHIEF

Which "Me" am I going to be?

Say you mentally (or actually) pull the DETECTIVE card. You can spend the meeting hunting out what's not being said, unearthing clues about what has happened or needs to. You don't need to put on the Poirot accent or wear a deerstalker. The point is not to play a detective, but to think like one. Say it's the JUDGE card, you'd bring all your sense of rightness and fairness to the discussion. The POET, the INVENTOR, the PHILOSOPHER ... They'd all have their effect on your thinking and behavior.

It's not hard. You just imagine yourself in the role and do what comes naturally. If in doubt, pretend.

Charlie Chaplin amazed fans by singing beautifully in his film *Modern Times*. "We didn't know you could sing, Charlie," they cooed. "I can't," he famously responded. "I am just imitating someone who can."

As a kid you had no difficulty playing different parts in your playground games, effortlessly switching from Godzilla to Sheriff, from Minnie Mouse to Cat Woman. Your mind is a database of alter-egos you can just reach into by imagining what "they" would do and doing it.

"But isn't that acting?" I remember one executive challenging me. He was concerned that this approach undermined his authenticity. Personally, I'd prefer inauthentic vitality to authentic deadness, but I didn't say that. What I said was that, if we are honest, we are *always acting*, in the sense that we are playing some version of ourselves.

The question for me is how inventive you are being. Are you consciously choosing the self you are playing at work? Or has it become habit?

And if you *are* choosing, how big is your repertoire?

Most people I see have a very narrow selection of selves to "wear" when they are at work—the ones they think are worklike, professional, and will make them look like a competent colleague. And they have been doing this so long that it has become automatic.

Dress Down Fridays and similar initiatives have gone some way to breaking down the dress code habits of big businesses. But changing pinstripes for chinos does not a revolution make. We need an equivalent to wean us off making thoughtless automatic choices of who we are going to be. It's not just that we check our personality at the door—as is often said. It is that we habitually put another one on.

This is why we came up with the mantra: *Bore No More.*

It's memorable. It rhymes. And it's right to the point. If you want to keep the interest of your colleagues (and customers), don't be predictable. Reliable, yes. But boringly typecast, no. Keep them guessing.

Meetings are great places to do this, to practice different versions of yourself and the effects they can have on others. You can do it for a tactical reason. For example, "I need to install the Negotiator today." Or you could do it for the hell of it. People don't quite know which you they are going to meet day by day? How exciting.

And why stop at work? Aren't there people in your personal life who would appreciate you broadening your repertoire? How about taking a friend or partner out for dinner and, before you sit down, installing one of your rarely seen and surprising "persions"? The Hedonist, perhaps? The Sensualist? The Sophisticate? The Incurable Romatic? The Adventurer? The Lover of Life? The Deeply Complex Mystery Guest? These are all you; the many, many yous.

Unexploded bombs and dealing with Hot Buttons

When you approach meetings the way I am suggesting, you create a richer, more dynamic mixture. The sparks will fly and occasionally things will explode. This is why you need to be aware of hot buttons, the unexploded ordnance of the modern meeting.

I have learned over many years of married life that if I dry my hands on the dishcloth I am in trouble with my wife. It means nothing to me. "Aren't they supposed to get dirty?" I reason with myself. But it means a lot to my wife. To her, me wiping my hands on a newly cleaned cloth means I do not appreciate all she does to keep the house in some kind of order. And this, in turn, means I do not respect or even really love her.

The dishcloth is what I call *a hot button* for my wife. It is an area of sensitivity that, if irritated, will create a disproportionate reaction. Most of us have these. But we tend to keep them to ourselves. This can turn a meeting into a minefield.

Fortunately there is a simple way to defuse the problem, without losing an arm or leg.

The way to uncover your colleagues' hot buttons is to *ask them*. I encourage all new teams to do this as part of laying the foundation for their working style—it's what I call their "User Guide."

Human beings don't come with an instruction manual, but if they did, it would certainly include information about how to avoid malfunctions and, worse, detonation.

I ask everyone in the team to think of themselves as a piece of equipment and to specify:

> *what its hot buttons are*
> *how to know if you have pressed one*
> *what to do about it*

Even hard-headed teams who will have no truck with the touchy-feely seem very happy go through the process of describing their hot buttons.

One CFO who comes to mind had a sensitivity about being interrupted while he was forming an idea. He was candid about this. But how were we to know if we had inadvertently tripped his hot button?

"That's easy," he replied. "I throw down my pen. Like a kid throwing his rattle out of his crib [his words not mine]."

Not only did he give us a clear signal but also a remedy. "If this happens, leave me be for a while so I can calm down. Then include me back into the conversation ... with humor. That usually does the trick."

I checked with the team a few months later and, apparently, the "pen signal" had been clearly picked up a few times and relationships had improved as a result. Interestingly, also, the pen was being thrown down less by our CFO. It was as if becoming more aware of this behavioral tick made it less necessary.

And this is a very important aspect of the "hot button" process. Yes, colleagues have a responsibility to be aware of your hot button and not to "press" it thoughtlessly. But you also have a responsibility to become aware of your sensitivity and find more helpful ways to respond if someone presses it than automatically blowing your top.

Before I leave this subject I just wanted to return to my wife. Like any partner, she has days when she feels more loved, and days when she feels less loved. My behavior will often have something to do with. But I won't always know. Unless I *ask*. So here's a revolutionary idea:

If you want your partner to feel more loved, find out what things make them feel loved—and do more of that.

It turns out that picking my wet towels up and putting them on the towel rail makes my wife feel more loved. Not hugely. But there is a definite effect. So the more I do it, the better.

I could try to achieve the same effect with a bunch of flowers or getting take-out Indian, but I'd be guessing. The towel is a sure-fire hit. How do I know? Because I asked her.

Is this something you could apply to your work?

Just ask your colleagues, customers, and clients what makes them feel more looked after, respected, valued, appreciated, powerful. And when they tell you, do more of that.

In work, in life, in meetings.

Psychic plumbing, the route to Effortless Rapport

One thing you need to know about humans. They all feel as if they are the only one. They know other people exist, of course, and they realize they are not actually the Only One on Earth. It just feels that way.

Each of us has an "I" that sits inside our bony and fleshy frame thinking it is the center of the universe. We have a whole set of beliefs and actions that support and bolster that point.

It's a very plausible position, just not very helpful when you are trying to connect with others. If you find yourself in a meeting feeling cut off from other people, try this next technique.

Imagine there's a pipe that runs out of the top of your head, through the ceiling (or along the airwaves if it's a virtual meeting) and down into the head of one of your colleagues. Do you feel more or less connected?

Now, every time they say something, imagine you know just what is going to come out of their mouth before they do. Imagine it's you saying it. How connected do you feel now?

Take it a step further and imagine you know what they are thinking. Imagine it's a two-way conduit, along which your thoughts and feelings can flow to them and back. How connected do you feel now? Watch what floats into your awareness.

If you practice this, you will, in my experience, find yourself being more intuitive about your colleagues. You start saying what was on their mind. It gets really exciting when you both come up with ideas simultaneously that are neither yours nor theirs but genuinely shared. This is a hallmark of high-quality connection.

272

And once you've built one pipe, there is nothing to stop you linking up the whole meeting with psychic plumbing.

It's pretty effortless when you get the hang of it, and the nice thing is, you're not actually connecting yourself to others, you're just reminding yourself how connected we already are.

Time for a Change

"The music is not in the notes but in the silence between."

Wolfgang Amadeus Mozart

We've looked at where you find the energy, but where will you find the time?

One of the things you will run up against whenever you attempt to make helpful changes is the "there's no time" mindset. You see it everywhere. Individuals use it, as do the organizations they work in, to justify not changing.

It seems plausible enough, but don't be taken in. When someone tells you they are too busy to work smarter, they are effectively saying, "I don't have time to save time."

The fact this excuse makes no sense doesn't stop people using it. I think this is partly because being busy has an enormously high premium in business. Busy-ness is where the modern term came from. Interestingly, the word derives from Old English *bisig*, which means anxiety. It appears that the stress that goes with being over-busy is nothing new.

We may have romantic notions of a past era when all was simple and the birds sang, but it appears that humans have been able to busy themselves into stress since the year zero. CT scan analysis of Egyptian mummies reveals atherosclerosis—a hardening of the arteries brought on by stress. And high levels of the stress hormone cortisol have been detected in the remains of ancient Peruvians.

My grandmotherly Italian neighbor Signora Anna once asked me what brought a London family to live in rural Italy. When I told her it was the slow pace of life, the *tranquillita*, she was perplexed and mildly amused. As I discovered when we got to know Piedmont better, life for her is every bit as busy as ours. You try maintaining a couple of acres of fruit orchard and vineyard by hand in a 24/7 battle with weather, insects, birds, pests, and airborne disease. Then there's the picking, the drying, the blanching, the boiling, the sieving, the straining, the canning. And we haven't even started to talk about the day-in day-out scrubbing, scouring, and bleaching of every domestic surface ... It's a pretty part of the world, yes. But stress free? Anything but.

As a race we like to be busy. And, much as we complain, we resist doing anything to make us less busy.

Saving time does actually take time. As the 17th-century philosopher Blaise Pascal famously wrote, apologizing for writing a long letter, "I didn't have time to write a short one." People plead for shorter PowerPoint presentations but, when it comes to it, you know that it's easier just to leave in all 60 slides than to boil them down to a pithy three. And when it comes to meetings, you have to make time to save time.

So where are we going to find this time?

The answer is—in the gaps.

I have a very busy client, Oscar, who is a leading international businessman. His schedule is twice as full as most of ours and yet Oscar remains composed. I was curious as to how he kept this sense of calm. Then, one day, I found myself on a conference call with him, waiting for the other participants to arrive. I was in London, he was in the back of a BMW 7 series in Frankfurt. As we waited, I asked him what he typically does during these lulls at the start of conference calls. There was a long pause and then he answered, with just two words: "I rest." Oscar was using the gaps between one engagement and another to hit the reset button.

It is something we can all do. Before, during, and after meetings there are gaps. They may only be short, but add them together and they mount up to considerable quantities of time you could be using to rest, reflect, think, prepare, invent ...

Just as, physicists tell us, at the subatomic level the universe is mostly space, even the fullest schedule is crammed with emptiness.

"I don't have time to breathe," the saying goes. And in meetings I have seen, that's literally true. People are so busy being busy they are forgetting to breathe. Breathing, when I last looked, was helpful to human life. It not only keeps the biological show on the road; properly used it can, quite literally, be a source of inspiration.

Countless wisdom traditions and self-development approaches—from yoga to martial arts—center on breathing. The common theme, as I have experienced it, goes something like this: *you have lungs, use them.* Calmer breathing calms your mind. Deep breathing deepens your thinking. You get the idea. Allowing breath into your lungs literally creates space in your body and metaphorically in your mind.

But there's more.

Mind the Gap

Have you noticed there is even a space between your breaths? Action-oriented animals as we are, we analyze breath by the two obvious actions—*breathing in* and *breathing out*. We even get busy breathing! But what about the space between the breaths? The moment when the body is neither inhaling or exhaling, but merely still?

Have a go now. I just clocked a normal cycle of in-breath-out-breath-in-breath at 12 seconds. And for seven of those I WAS DOING NOTHING AT ALL. My body was enjoying the oxygen I had thoughtfully provided for it while collecting up unwanted CO_2 to exhale. But my breathing was still. And when I notice that, I become still.

Imagine you are throwing a tennis ball up in the air. It goes up and then comes down. But if you rewind and look closely, there is a moment when it is neither rising nor falling. It is hanging in space. In the gap between actions, there is a moment when the ball isn't doing anything at all.

I like to think all our daily activities have these mini-breaks hidden within them. The more you notice it, the more of them you get. It's a bit like peering at an apparently solid object through a powerful microscope and finding it's mostly empty space.

You can do the same with your day. Take a look at your diary. In between all the blocks of stuff you have put in, there are gaps. And even within the calls, deals, and meetings, there are thousands of gaps.

When you start noticing these gaps you start to find time in your day. And you can use that valuable time to make the changes you want to make.

Before the call ...

Remember the anatomy of a real meeting. Bring to mind *why* you are making this call and picture the outcome you want. See the *other callers* in your mind's eye—as well as the *bigger picture* that surrounds the meeting. Finally, as you dial in, remind yourself of any *content* points. With a bit of practice that should take you ten seconds, no more. I don't care how busy and/or important you are. You have ten seconds.

In the meeting ...

If you are wise you won't be overstuffing your meetings with content, but even if you have fallen back into bad ways and the content is jammed back-to-back on the agenda, there is always time in the gaps.

What you see on the page is not what happens in reality. The printed agenda may look full, with items butted together like seamless breeze blocks. But the reality is, however much territory has been staked out in the agenda, the prime real estate is the links between the items. This is why I always counsel the meeting leader to *own the links*. The links are where the leader can steer the meeting, prompt reflection, add meaning, summarize important points, re-energize a flagging conversation.

When a client shoves an over-busy meeting design in my face, I spend my time looking at the ink-lines between the items, imagining the deft and mischievous things we can do with these slivers of time.

NEXT STEPS: DON'T LET HARRY MISS SALLY

Earlier I suggested that the mischievous meeting revolutionary should hijack the summary. And that's precisely what I am going to do here.

I could be looking back at all we've covered; at the differences between nearly meeting and really meeting; the why, who, how, and what of real meeting design; at those seven archetypal meetings that form the basis of your meeting palette; at some mischievous ideas about how to change meeting practice and make those changes stick.

I could be asking "what specifically was of value to you?" and "what would have been even more valuable?" These are two great questions with which to end your meetings, by the way, as they encourage people to extract the value of the meeting and keep it in mind. I could even weave in a list of to-dos, of actions to be completed by the time we next meet.

I could, but I won't. Instead, I want to leave you with a question.

"What if Harry hadn't met Sally?"

If you don't know the film *When Harry Met Sally*, it's a romantic comedy where Meg Ryan and Billy Crystal play a couple of best friends who fall in love—finally—decades after they first meet. It's a touch-and-go thing. Boy very nearly loses Girl. But if they'd never met in the first place, they'd have had no chance. All of that potential would have been lost.

It's the sort of thing I find myself wondering. What if Ben had missed Jerry? Would we have Rocky Road or Phish Food? How would Procter have fared without Gamble? And what if Dolce had been out when Gabbana came to call?

Where would the world be now if Ronald Reagan had said *no* to meeting Mikhail Gorbachev, or if Ian Paisley and the Loyalists hadn't finally sat down with Gerry Adams and the Republicans in Northern Ireland to settle their differences? What would the world be like if Nelson Mandela hadn't secretly met for tea with P.W. Botha on July 5 1989 to pave the way for peaceful transition to Black Majority Rule? From the moment the notoriously white-supremacist president poured tea for his black revolutionary guest both men knew, as Mandela later wrote in his autobiography, "there was no turning back."

If Steve Jobs hadn't bumped into Steve Wozniak I would probably be writing this in longhand, not on a gorgeous Apple laptop.

NEXT STEPS: DON'T LET HARRY MISS SALLY

If Mr. Marks and Mr. Spencer hadn't sat down together then—
whoosh—that's my underwear gone. If John Lennon hadn't crea-
tively meshed with Paul McCartney in Liverpool we'd be living
today with no "Yesterday."

There's an endless list of ways our world would be poorer if
people had missed rather than met.

And that leads me to speculate about the meetings that aren't
happening that should be.

The North Koreans clearly need some sort of serious powwow
with the South Koreans. A real meeting is long overdue between
the Israelis and Palestinians. The sooner the various fundamen-
talists around the world settle their differences with the rest of
us, the better. And it looks like the world's leaders need to sit
down and really crack this future of the planet thing; not with
a "nearly meeting" like the Climate Change Conference in
Copenhagen or Durban, but a real one. I understand from people
wiser than myself that there are about 20 key problems for
humanity to crack and they are all solvable if we could talk across
boundaries rather than pursuing our own narrow interests.

If real meetings were happening all over the world, what could
we *not* create? What conflicts could be avoided? What great new
ideas could we collectively have that we'd individually miss? If
only we weren't so busy nearly meeting ...

And what about you? What meetings would you like to see
happen? And what could you do to make that a reality?

Now you are killing off those nearly meetings—or just about
to—you're going to have much more time for the real meetings
you really want to have. Think of something you really want to

achieve with the time you have left in this life and imagine a meeting that would help that happen.

Think about work.

Whom do you need to sit down with that you have been avoiding? What's the most powerful group you could get together to answer the current big questions? What isn't being said, and why don't you stage a meeting where it can be talked about? Whom or what haven't you met to celebrate? And isn't it high time you did?

Think closer to home.

Every family seems to have its pockets of non-communication (or is that just mine?). What about some really meeting, so that close relatives can be just that? And then there are the friends—the real ones, not the Twitterati. What about finding some real time in our busy lives for these irreplaceable people, instead of just skittering over the surface when we see each other?

If you could invite anyone to a "fantasy meeting" who would they be and what would you discuss?

Imagine you're sitting at a table with seven empty chairs and you can fill them any way you want. Personally, I'd be curious to see how Placido Domingo, Aung San Suu Kyi, Bill Bryson, Martin Scorsese, Emma Thompson, and Muhammad Yunus would get along with each other. I'd love to know what life has taught them and to see what we could create together over some great food and wine.

When you start to exercise your capacities to really meet, rather than just organize a meeting, you'll find even the ordinary day is full of possibilities we are currently walking straight past.

NEXT STEPS: DON'T LET HARRY MISS SALLY

How well do you know the people living on your own street? At the time of the 2010 elections in the U.K. there was much talk of the Big Society and the value of local community. One friend of mine, Dr. Nick Buckley, decided to turn rhetoric into experiment. He drew a one-mile circle around the manhole cover in his front garden and now dedicates a day a week to really meeting the people who share his "square mile" with him. (OK, technically it's a *circular* mile ...) What real meetings await discovery a stone's throw from your house?

The space between home and work turns out to be a very fertile ground for you to practice your meeting technique. I have recently been developing a project with the U.S.-based Wisdom University that we call "Street Wisdom" (www.streetwisdom.org), which is designed to help us turn the street into a learning zone. You'd be amazed by what you start to notice and the people you meet when you take the time to slow down and connect with what's really happening around you.

One of the glorious things about the chance meetings you have on the street is that no one knows who you are. So you can practice being different people, or different versions of yourself.

At home I play Husband, Father, and (very) occasionally DIY Superhero. At work I am an Entrepreneur and "Creative." But what about the space in between? On a good day there are 40 minutes between home and my office during which I tend to take the "role" of any normal London commuter. I squeeze myself into crammed spaces. I avoid the gaze of my fellow travelers. I play games on my iPhone while pretending to read email. It's dull. So I have recently started to break the pattern and try different versions—upgrades of the DP software, if you like. I have experimented so far with Spy, Poet, Social Provocateur, Student of the Human Condition, Good Samaritan, Clairvoyant, Meditator, International Man of Mystery, and Fashion Icon. The last one was a bit of a stretch. Forty minutes, twice a day, builds into a monumental 37 days a year when I am free to be whoever I say I am. And that's before I even get to work.

Some of the best real meetings don't even require anyone else to show up. The Zen teacher Genpo Roshi is a wonderfully engaging communicator who manages to make some of the mysteries of Zen philosophy accessible to the wider world without you having to sit on a cold, hard mat for twenty years. He likens human beings to a corporation with many departments and functions, all jostling for control. Getting all those factions to work together is a real challenge—especially when the CEO appears to be away on an extended golf trip. Inspired by his Big Mind process I have spent hours of enlightening fun getting the different "voices" in my head to stop squabbling and really meet each other. I recommend it.

When you give yourself freedom to play different versions of yourself, you not only see the world differently, it sees you differently. You'll meet unexpected people and have surprising conversations.

Anyone who likes foreign travel and has a bit of thirst for adventure knows the difference between *commuting* and really *traveling*. As travelers we tend to be much more open to sights, sounds, strangers and their stories, than we are on a routine trip to the mall. We hop on planes to faraway places in search of adventurous encounters and ignore those staring us in the face at home. The amount of adventure you are having depends on your mindset, not your location.

I remember sitting next to a CEO client on a very ordinary bench on a street in Central London. We were on a "street quest" to improve his connection with others. This included him sketching a stranger in a café opposite. He wasn't thrilled by this idea initially ("I can't draw, I am not artistic; I'm a numbers man, not a visual person," etc.). However, we persisted and he found he actually enjoyed himself. Then I suggested he cross the street, introduce himself to the person he had been sketching, and give them his portrait as a gift. You should have seen the look on his face. It was as though we were on some extreme team-building event and I had asked him to bungee-jump head-first off a suspension bridge into some white-water rapids. Actually I think he would have preferred to take that challenge than those few steps. But, all credit to him, he did it and the stranger was pleased, even touched, by this unexpected gesture. The whole exercise took a few minutes, but it is a meeting that I bet neither of them will forget.

How often is a real meeting, a fascinating conversation, an intriguing new person, a life-changing memory, just a few steps away? And why don't we take those few steps?

I can't speak for other cultures, but here in the North of Europe where I grew up, we often feel like it's impolite to take the initiative. We'd rather not risk looking silly, pushy, intrusive, and so we let opportunities pass. It's as if we are waiting for an invitation to meet life.

But revolutions rarely start with an invitation. They start when someone takes the initiative.

So, if there's just one message in this book I'd want you to take away, it is this:

> *The difference between nearly meeting and really meeting is—you.*

Yes, good design helps make a real meeting more likely. So does picking the right people, creating a powerful context and selecting the right content. The technologies in this book will be very helpful, but only when you make real meeting your intention. Intention trumps every technique, tool, and trick.

If you genuinely want real meetings, you'll find you start taking the initiative, whether you are leading them or not. You'll find yourself less and less tolerant of nearly meetings. And donuts will no longer be sufficient incentive to put up with them. If you take a lead, others will follow. Believe me, your colleagues are every bit as fed up as you when meetings are tedious, irrelevant, boring, wasteful, ineffective, and/or inefficient.

That's how revolutions begin. With small steps. Like a hesitant businessman crossing a city street to give a child-like sketch to a stranger.

We began the book talking about the humble meeting as a way of "revolutionizing business." But once we get the hang of it, why would we want to stop there?

NEXT STEPS: DON'T LET HARRY MISS SALLY

Your society, your community, your colleagues, friends, and families—they'll all benefit when you become passionate about "really meeting."

When you start looking, you'll find opportunities for really meeting are everywhere. Start taking those opportunities and we *will* change the world.

And when we do? The donuts are on me!

YOUR REAL MEETING CHECKLIST

Ten things the Real Meeting Revolutionary should know:

1. Every meeting is "your" meeting

When you turn from victim to revolutionary, every meeting is a chance to change things, whether you are officially leading it or not.

2. Fewer meetings, more meeting

Don't arrange a formal meeting when an informal meeting will do.

3. There is no such thing as "a meeting"

There are seven basic reasons to meet (at least) and each requires a very different approach.

4. If you don't know why you are in a meeting, *don't* be in the meeting

5. If you can't improve a bad meeting ...

... make it worse until even your most conservative colleagues realize things have got to change.

6. When you are done, stop—whatever the schedule says

Life never happens in hour-long chunks. Stop working for your diary organizer and get it working for you.

7. Meetings need to be led. That's ALL meetings

If no one else is leading, the leader is *you*.

8. Bad meetings always have "good" reasons

Until you understand what people are getting from a bad meeting, they won't change.

9. Create value

The most important design question you can ask is "How does this meeting create extraordinary value for everyone involved?"

10. The Revolution starts today

Don't wait for a printed invitation. Now's the time to start killing off all those bad meetings so there's space for a few great ones.

11.* Bore no more!

This book isn't about boring meetings and whether you want to have them, it's about boring lives and whether you want to live one.

---

* *Because a Top Ten list with only ten items really would be boring.*

LET'S STAY CONNECTED

Join the Real Meeting Revolution at:

www.willtherebedonuts.com

And take our **free test** that helps you calculate exactly what you and your company are wasting on "nearly" meetings.

For more information on David Pearl and his inspiring work with businesses, please contact:

Pearl Group
info@pearlgroup.net
t: +44 (208) 439 5765
www.pearlgroup.net

Follow David on Twitter @davidpearlhere